The Flow Factor

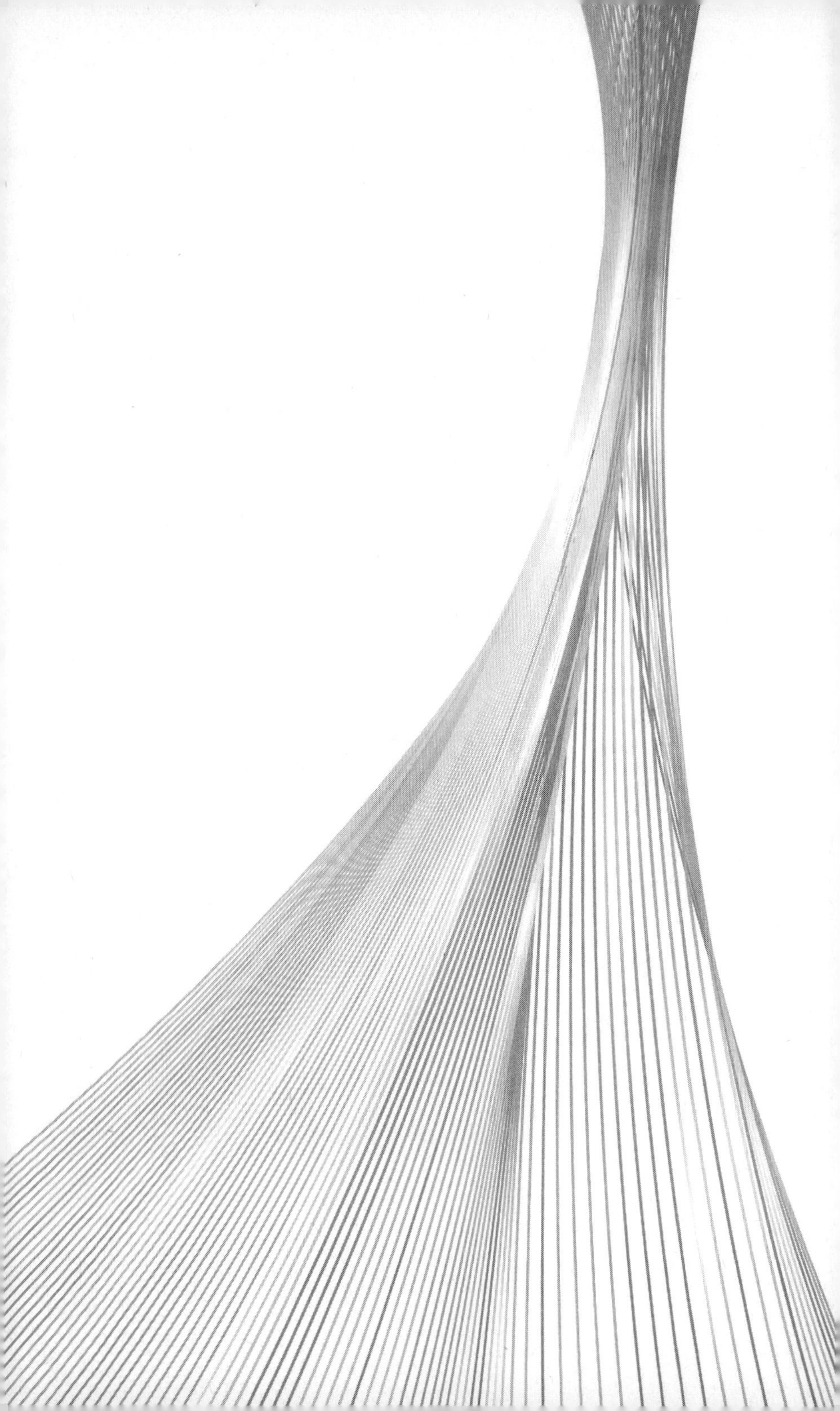

HOW TO MASTER YOUR ENERGY
AND ENTER A STATE OF FLOW

The Flow Factor

CHRISTY WHITMAN
New York Times **Bestselling Author**

BEYOND WORDS
Portland, Oregon

BEYOND WORDS
1750 S.W. Skyline Blvd., Suite 20
Portland, Oregon 97221-2543
503-531-8700 / 503-531-8773 fax
www.beyondword.com

First Beyond Words paperback edition September 2025
Copyright © 2025 by Christy Whitman
All rights reserved, including the right to reproduce this book or portions thereof in any form.

This publication contains the opinions and ideas of its author. It is intended to provide helpful and informative material on the subjects addressed in the publication. It is sold with the understanding that the author and publisher are not engaged in rendering medical, health, or any other kind of personal professional services in the book. The reader should consult his or her medical, health, or other competent professional before adopting any of the suggestions in this book or drawing inferences from it. The author and publisher specifically disclaim all responsibility for any liability, loss, or risk, personal or otherwise, which is incurred as a consequence, directly or indirectly, of the use and application of any of the contents of this book.

BEYOND WORDS PUBLISHING and colophon are registered trademarks of Beyond Words Publishing.
Beyond Words is an imprint of Simon & Schuster, LLC.

For more information about special discounts for bulk purchases, please contact Beyond Words Special Sales at 503-531-8700 or specialsales@beyondword.com.

Managing editor: Lindsay Easterbrooks-Brown
Editors: Michele Ashtiani Cohn, Bailey Potter
Copyeditor: Kristin Thiel
Proofreader: Ashley Van Winkle
Design: Sara E. Blum
Composition: William H. Brunson Typography Services

Manufactured in the United States of America

10 9 8 7 6 5 4 3 2 1

Library of Congress Cataloging-in-Publication Data:

Names: Whitman, Christy author
Title: The flow factor : how to master your energy and enter a state of flow / Christy Whitman.
Description: First Beyond Words paperback edition. | Portland, Oregon : Beyond Words, 2025. | Includes bibliographical references.
Identifiers: LCCN 2025006524 (print) | LCCN 2025006525 (ebook) | ISBN 9781582709383 paperback | ISBN 9781582709390 ebook
Subjects: LCSH: Success | Self-actualization (Psychology)
Classification: LCC BF637.S8 W446 2025 (print) | LCC BF637.S8 (ebook) | DDC 158.1—dc23/eng/20250530
LC record available at https://lccn.loc.gov/2025006524
LC ebook record available at https://lccn.loc.gov/2025006525

The corporate mission of Beyond Words Publishing, Inc.: *Inspire to Integrity*

To every single human who will inevitably
experience contrast in their life.

To both the multimillionaires and those
who feel like they don't have anything . . .

Your feelings are real.

Your thoughts are real.

What you are going through is real.

My question to you is, do you want to continue with your current reality, or do you want to create a new reality for yourself?

This book will show you how to change your entire reality,
if you let it.

Have fun!

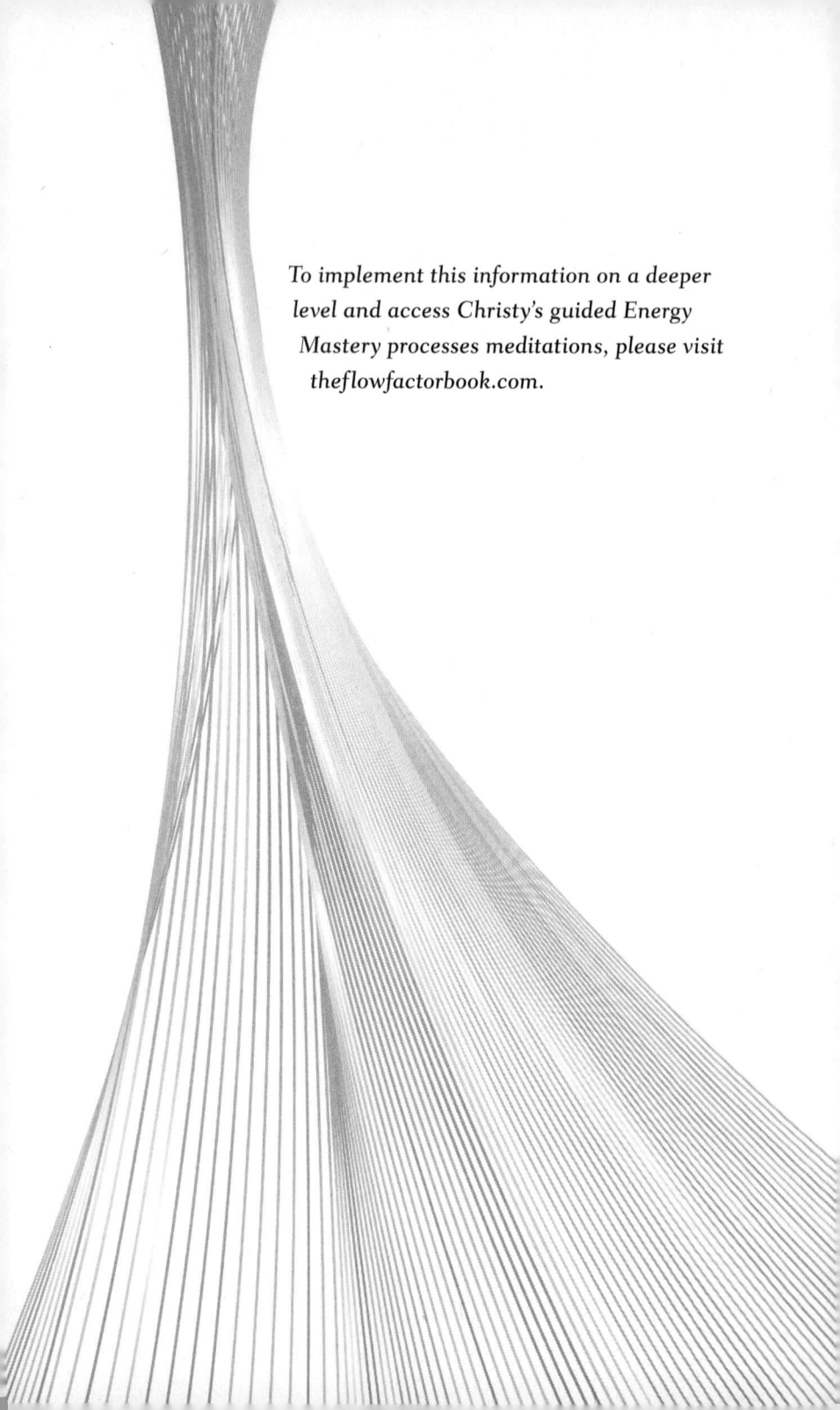

To implement this information on a deeper level and access Christy's guided Energy Mastery processes meditations, please visit theflowfactorbook.com.

CONTENTS

Foreword by Mary Morrissey ix

Preface xiii

Introduction xvii

1 The Source of Flow 1

2 Unlocking the Power of Your Free Will 15

3 Faces of Resistance: Fight, Flight, Freeze, and Fawn 39

4 Energetic Imprints and Emotional Triggers 61

5 Contrast as an Invitation to Energy Mastery 87

Conclusion 105

Appendix: Energy Mastery Processes to Move from
   Resistance to Flow 109

Resources 143

Selected Bibliography 147

Acknowledgments 149

About the Author 151

FOREWORD

I fell in love with Christy Whitman the first time I met her. I conduct interviews on a regular basis on the topics of spirituality and self-development. There was something special about Christy and her passion for transforming lives. After she interviewed me, she felt guided to ask me if I would mentor her; it was a big yes for me even though I wasn't offering that kind of coaching at the time. This was in 2012, and since then, Christy and I have become good friends as well as avid supporters of one another's work. Christy and I are both transformational leaders, authors, and coaches, and in any traditional business model we'd be considered competitors. The fact that we've maintained a very open and collaborative relationship for all these years speaks to the message at the very heart of this book.

Whether we're aware of it or not, most of us are living pretty guarded and limited lives. Of course we have dreams and desires, but as soon as these bubble up from within us, they are almost instantly drowned out by the familiar voice of worry and doubt that tells us, *Watch out. Don't get hurt again. There's not enough to go around, so defend what's yours.* These conditioned responses might masquerade

Foreword

as protectors of our tender hearts, but in reality, they're more like prison guards, locking us inside a life of contraction and repetition. As I sometimes joke with my coaching clients, if we spend the majority of our time imagining the impossible, we're sure to achieve it. Within the realm of what we already know, there can be no innovation, no genuine inspiration, no magic. It's only when we're brave enough to step outside of the limitations that we construct that we do what I consider to be the greatest use of this lifetime: fully express our unique gifts, create a life filled with meaning and fulfillment, and contribute our energy to something larger than ourselves. In other words, we transcend the world of the mundane and enter the world of flow.

As I'm sure you've noticed, Life is always changing and expanding, always pressing us to become more. Nothing stands still. This is as true for a blade of grass as it is for a galaxy, and it's certainly true for you and me. Maybe you've also noticed, longing and discontent are the alerts that Life sends to reach us, to wake us from our trance of repetition and nudge us toward authentic self-expression, abundance, and freedom. The question is, what is our response to Life's inevitable nudges?

If we cling to a fixed mindset, we cement ourselves to the very conditions we're struggling against. *The Flow Factor* guides you toward a growth mindset from which you begin to understand that encountering Life's challenges is essential to your evolution as a human being. Only when you come face-to-face with adversity on your way to something that's really important to you do you reach in and find your innate power to flow your creative energy—regardless of circumstances—and discover what you are really made of.

Rather than fixating on the details of the circumstances that surround you, this book will help you to turn your gaze toward the powerful flow of energy that orchestrated those circumstances into being and to realize that this power is also within you. Flow can't be forced, manipulated, or bargained with, but it can be invited and allowed. The energy mastery processes found throughout this book will support you in soothing the reactive patterns of thought and emotion that keep you weighed down by fear and self-doubt so that you're more available to receive the nudges toward your own greatness that Life is sending your way. Christy is an excellent teacher and shares many spiritual truths within these pages, which you can use to bring greater ease and abundance to your human experience.

You have taken birth in a human body, and therefore have a front-row ticket to one of the greatest shows in all the universe. You are simultaneously human and divine, born into a limited body, yet aware that you are an unlimited and unbounded spirit. The opportunity before you is unparalleled. There are powerful universal forces at play beyond the realm of form and circumstance, and these forces are yours to create with when you open up to the realm of flow. This book will show you the way.

—Mary Morrissey
bestselling author of *Brave Thinking*
and *Building Your Field of Dreams*

PREFACE

Have you ever lost yourself in the magic of a perfect moment? A moment when thoughts of all kinds melted away and you felt resourceful, in command, and at one with everything and everyone around you? Have you had the experience of watching something you desire unfold effortlessly, without hard work or struggle but with a feeling of awe and even elation? These are all glimpses of flow—a state of heightened focus, creativity, and joy, where time seems to stand still and possibilities are endless. If you haven't experienced this, this book will assist you in reaching this state of flow, and if you have achieved this state of being, this book will help you expand it even further.

At the most basic level, flow state feels like ease. You're no longer fighting the river by paddling upstream but simply letting go and allowing the current to carry you, trusting that everything you want is waiting for you downstream. Flow feels like being in the right place at the right time, like things are falling into place without a lot of effort, as though they were being orchestrated by some broader intelligence. In flow state—conversationally referred to as being "in the zone"—your body is relaxed, your mind is calm yet responsive, and you have the emotional and psychological resources to skillfully navigate any situation life brings your way. Flow is a state of supreme adaptability that allows you to make the very best of any situation you find yourself in, like a master chef who can make a delicious meal from whatever ingredients are on hand.

For as many times as you've experienced flow, I'm sure that you have also experienced its opposite. Maybe you've gone through periods of feeling frustrated or resigned because the outcomes you've been working toward haven't yet come to fruition. Or maybe you've had the experience of cruising through life, feeling great and flying high, only to bump against something—a piece of bad news, a tense interaction, an aggravating delay, or even a self-critical thought—that abruptly tossed you out of flow state. If you're like most people, you instantly became aware that your personal vibration has just taken a nosedive, but you're less clear about how it happened or how to get back into alignment. Truth be told, many of us are living in a state of chronic stress, our bodies on high alert and our minds perpetually agitated and reactive. For most of us, flow state—if we experience it at all—is fleeting and unpredictable.

Throughout my twenty-five-year career as an author, energy healer, and the founder of an international coaching academy that has certified more than three thousand coaches worldwide, I have discovered two things about the Flow Factor. First, that flow is not a result of luck, circumstance, money, or status but a vibrational state that all of us can learn to access, anytime and anywhere. Second, that mastery of our own mental, emotional, and physical energies is the key to accessing the state of flow—and therefore the key to experiencing ease, happiness, and success in all aspects of life.

Through my books, workshops, and coaching programs, I have taught tens of thousands of people all over the world to consciously direct their energy to create the outcomes they desire by choosing their thoughts, emotions, perspectives, attitudes, and reactions on purpose. I've coached people who are now experiencing relief from a lifetime of migraines and physical pain. I've worked with those who are now medication-free, having restored the natural state of equilibrium between body, mind, and spirit. I've had many clients who first came to me with a vague business idea or faint inner calling and who have reinvented their careers and are now thriving—financially, yes, but also in every other sense of the word. Everything I share is for the purpose of supporting others in keeping their mental, emotional, physical, and energy bodies open and flowing, even as they move through the painful or unwanted experiences that are an inevitable part of life.

I myself have moved through many unwanted life experiences, such as divorce, several mountains of debt, losing a job, my newborn son having open-heart surgery, and the death of loved ones, including my sister who died by suicide. At each of these turning points—and using the processes and techniques I'll share with you throughout this book—I made the necessary internal adjustments to process the trauma so I could again refocus my creative energies on what I desire, what I appreciate, and what I want to experience more of. In other words, instead of developing PTSD, I developed post-traumatic *growth*. This book is the culmination of all my experience to date and, in fact, extends far beyond the realm of my own personal experience.

Just after publishing my sixth book, *Quantum Success*, I became a conscious energy conduit and messenger for a group of ascended masters who call themselves The Quantum Council of Light. Although I have been receiving from the Council for many decades—and my very first book was "given" to me in a series of messages I received in the middle of the night for seven consecutive nights—in September 2018, the Council came through me in a way that they never had before. The words and energy transmissions I receive through the Council are beyond anything that I, Christy Whitman, could ever conceive of on my own, and I am beyond grateful for the influx of their energy in my life and work. All the meditations and hands-on energy mastery processes you will find in the appendix of this book came directly from The Quantum Council of Light.

Early on in my relationship with the Council, while feeling overwhelmed by the power of their message, I asked, "Why me?" They replied simply, "Why *not* you?" What I now realize is that my continued willingness to release my resistance to life's challenges and to focus on what I want and how I want to feel has made me much more open, intuitive, and receptive to the flow of divine guidance that underlies every situation and event. It is my deepest desire that you use this book as your own personal guide to master your energy, release your resistance, and align with the Flow Factor in every aspect of your life.

INTRODUCTION

Mastery of your own energy field, of your own personal vibration, is the ultimate measure of success.

Think of it this way: How successful are you really if at any moment someone or something can knock you off balance, steal your peace of mind, or chip away at your faith and your inner knowing that all is well with you and with life? How much can you enjoy the sweetness of any of the manifestations that surround you if you're just one thought away from a racing pulse or a nagging sense of unease? And how deep can your happiness run if a contrasting event—as trivial as receiving an offhand comment from someone you love or a rude look from a perfect stranger—can send you spiraling into a fit of agitation, insecurity, or fear?

I was first introduced to the concept of *contrast* in the late 1990s though the teachings of Abraham, a collective consciousness of nonphysical energies interpreted by Esther Hicks. Contrast, as Abraham explains in *Ask and It Is Given*, refers to any unwanted situation or condition that evokes painful emotions within us. Put simply, contrast is experiencing anything that you do not want. While most people view contrast as something to avoid, it is a critical part of any creative process. It is only through the contrast of living with what you don't want that you become clear about the kind of life you desire to create.

Contrast comes in many forms. Infinite, in fact. From tragic, life-altering events to petty annoyances, contrast is an inescapable part of our human experience. No amount of money, education, or privilege can shield us from unwanted experiences like stress, uncertainty, loss, or death. Even if we opted to live on a mountaintop or in a cave and our only relationships were with birds and other wildlife, we would still encounter contrast. Grief is universal, just as love, appreciation, and joy are universal. As my grandfather used to say, "Nobody gets out of this alive." Even the experience of achieving a long-desired goal is shadowed with contrast, because in gaining something wanted, we simultaneously open ourselves up to the possibility of losing it or eventually growing dissatisfied with the achievement and wondering, *Is this all there is?*

All of these unwanted or polarizing experiences are an integral part of life because life itself is polarity. Consider the fact that the entire universe of which we are a part was created through the interaction of opposing and contrasting forces, relying on the balance found between them: up and down, empty and full, gaining and losing, pleasure and pain. Most of us encounter hundreds of "threats" to our vibrational stability every single day, from the driver who flips us off in traffic, to a rude or negative comment made about us on social media, to the rising price of a pint of milk or a gallon of gas, to the ping of a phone notification warning of an impending deadline. While most of these are not immediate or even eventual threats to our survival, many of us react as though our lives are on the line.

Introduction

Degrees of Contrast: Big-T and Little-T Traumas

Trauma is a heavy word, but the fact is that every one of us has been shaped by our experiences, just as we are influenced by our daily interactions with family, friends, coworkers, and neighbors. Later in this book, I'll give you the formal definition of *trauma*, and we'll explore the works of people like Francine Shapiro, the psychologist who popularized the concepts of *Big-T trauma* and *little-t trauma* nearly fifty years ago.

For now, you can think of these two types of traumas like this: Experiences like suffering a serious injury, sexual violence, a physical threat, or abuse, abandonment, or rejection by someone we love, and other life-threatening events like experiencing war, combat, and natural disasters, fall into the category of Big-T traumas, which clearly shape our identities and shake our sense of stability. Little-t traumas are those common, garden-variety situations that most, if not all, of us experience on a regular basis—things like social isolation, financial pressures, strained relationships, job loss, and chronic stress. These little-t traumas may not meet the clinical criteria for acute trauma, but they can still have significant negative impacts on our mental health and well-being—in other words, they can still quickly take us out of flow state and into survival mode.

Now, I am neither an MD nor a trauma expert, but I have spent the last twenty-five years coaching people from every walk of life, and I have seen countless examples of what happens when we allow Big-T and little-t traumas to pile up without processing the energy of these experiences. We may move on from the event itself, but unless we have the tools to release the energy triggered by the experience, we continue to live in that same low-level vibration of sadness, anger, and powerlessness.

Introduction

When we're carrying around the unprocessed emotional energy of disappointment, pain, worry, doubt, and fear, we re-create the same type of unsatisfying experiences and dynamics, either with the same people or with a changing cast of characters. We may be living in a grown-up body, but emotionally and energetically, we operate in the world like a wounded four-year-old. Rather than living in a state of flow where we feel receptive, resourceful, and well-situated within life's unfolding, we feel stuck in a chronic vibration of fear and reactivity.

Stuck in Survival Mode

Whenever we're faced with a situation that we perceive as a threat, our nervous system automatically activates one of four primitive survival responses: *fight, flight, freeze,* or *fawn*. In actuality, psychologists have identified a total of six survival responses, but the additional two, *flop* and *friend*, are variations of the *freeze* and *fawn* responses. These survival states, rooted far back in our evolutionary history, are hardwired into us to protect us from danger. Even though most of the events that trigger our body's powerful survival responses are not actual emergencies in the same way that running from a hungry tiger or being in a true state of starvation are emergencies, our nervous system still registers them, and then reacts to them, as threats.

Once our survival responses have been activated, we become like a puppet on someone else's string, no longer in control of our perceptions or our reactions. Our primitive nervous system hijacks our broader awareness, spiraling us into a state of hypervigilance and diverting all our available energy, resources, and attention to surviving the perceived threat. With our primitive survival instincts engaged, few inner resources are available to support the rest, repair, and renewal of our body and mind, and fewer still are left over to

Introduction

promote our growth and evolution, the expansion of our wisdom, or the enhancement of our life experience—aka, the pursuit of our happiness and success.

Until we gain mastery over our own nervous systems, which means mastery of our own energy, we are nothing but slaves to our basest survival instincts, reacting to life rather than creating our lives, finding ourselves forever at the mercy of other people and external circumstances. Feeling no control over the quality of our own life experience, we cling desperately to life's pleasures while trying to avoid its pain. This leaves us prone to vices of all kinds as we seek to quiet our growing sense of powerlessness. So, there is contrast, and there is our resistance to contrast, and these are two very different things.

This book will guide you to greater awareness and resourcefulness in those critical moments between a trigger and your reaction to it. It will show you how to appreciate the value of contrast, manage your own resistance to it, and get back into a flow of energy that feels good, so that you can move toward what you desire with ease.

Our journey begins in chapter one with an exploration of the energetic universe in which we live because it is our alignment with this stream of intelligent energy that determines how much or little flow we experience in any moment. This invisible flow of life force energy, often referred to as Source, is the origin of all manifested things. It's the force that animates everything from the smallest atom to the vast cosmos, the source of all abundance and inspiration. The human body is both an extension of and a conduit for this stream of energy, and when we're in alignment with its flow, we experience joy, peace, and fulfillment.

In chapter two, we consider the role that free will plays in our moment-to-moment relationship with flow. The frequencies of struggle, drama, chaos, and lack reside at one end of the spectrum of our consciousness, the energy of ease, abundance, and flow at the

Introduction

other. Our free will is what determines which end of this scale we resonate on. This means that in every moment, we get to decide whether to give in to the fear, negativity, despair, and cynicism that surround us or to exercise our innate power to choose and reclaim our position as the creator, the attractor, and the allower of everything that flows into our life experience.

In chapter three, we examine the five facets of our waking consciousness—perception, thoughts, feelings, words, and actions—and explore how the current state of each one impacts our experience of flow. This chapter also provides a detailed description of each of our primitive survival states to help you identify which primary survival instinct—fighting, fleeing, freezing, or fawning—is most dominantly wired within you.

In chapter four, we consider the role that our energetic imprints and emotional triggers play in blocking our moment-to-moment access to flow. Regardless of the relative ease or difficulty of our childhoods, we all come away from them wired with unique patterns of resistance and reactivity. In the yoga philosophy, these are known as samskaras, the subtle impressions that remain in our energy fields as the result of unhealed past experiences. When these pockets of resistance are triggered—even by something relatively trivial—we may find ourselves acting out in the most primitive of ways, unable to uphold our boundaries or regulate our own energy streams, often flying into uncontrollable fits of anxiety, overwhelm, or rage. Then, later, after the emotional trigger has subsided, we may slip into self-condemnation, wondering why we lost our cool, didn't express our desires, or failed to listen to our intuition—yet again.

In chapter five, we explore contrasting or challenging life experiences as powerful catalysts that—once understood—can allow us to surrender more deeply into flow. The survival instincts that grip us when we find ourselves face-to-face with a painfully unwanted situation serve a divine purpose: They show us where our individual energy stream is out of alignment with the universal flow of life. This chapter will support you in softening your resistance to contrast by understanding the essential role that it plays in all growth and evolution.

Finally, in the book's appendix, I'll share some specific energy mastery processes to help you release the energetic blocks stored within your mental and emotional bodies that obstruct the stream of intuition and intelligence that is always attempting to guide you back to flow. With practice, you will become skilled at neutralizing your internal resistance and will be better able to choose the direction of ease, abundance, and flow, even in high-stakes situations. As a result of this sequential journey, my intent for you is that you remember, even amid contrast, that the Flow Factor is always available to you and that you understand how to find the path to rejoining it.

The highest accomplishment in life is knowing that you have within you the power to flow your energy as you wish, toward the outcomes that you desire, regardless of—or even in direct contradiction to—whatever may be happening around you. Real success is owning your innate ability to carry within you the vibration of stability, safety, joy, and prosperity, even when entering an environment where none of those things are present. The freedom we all seek does not come from securing just the right set of circumstances, and it cannot come from successfully outrunning contrast. It comes only from knowing that each of us—and no one else—is in control of our own energy flow.

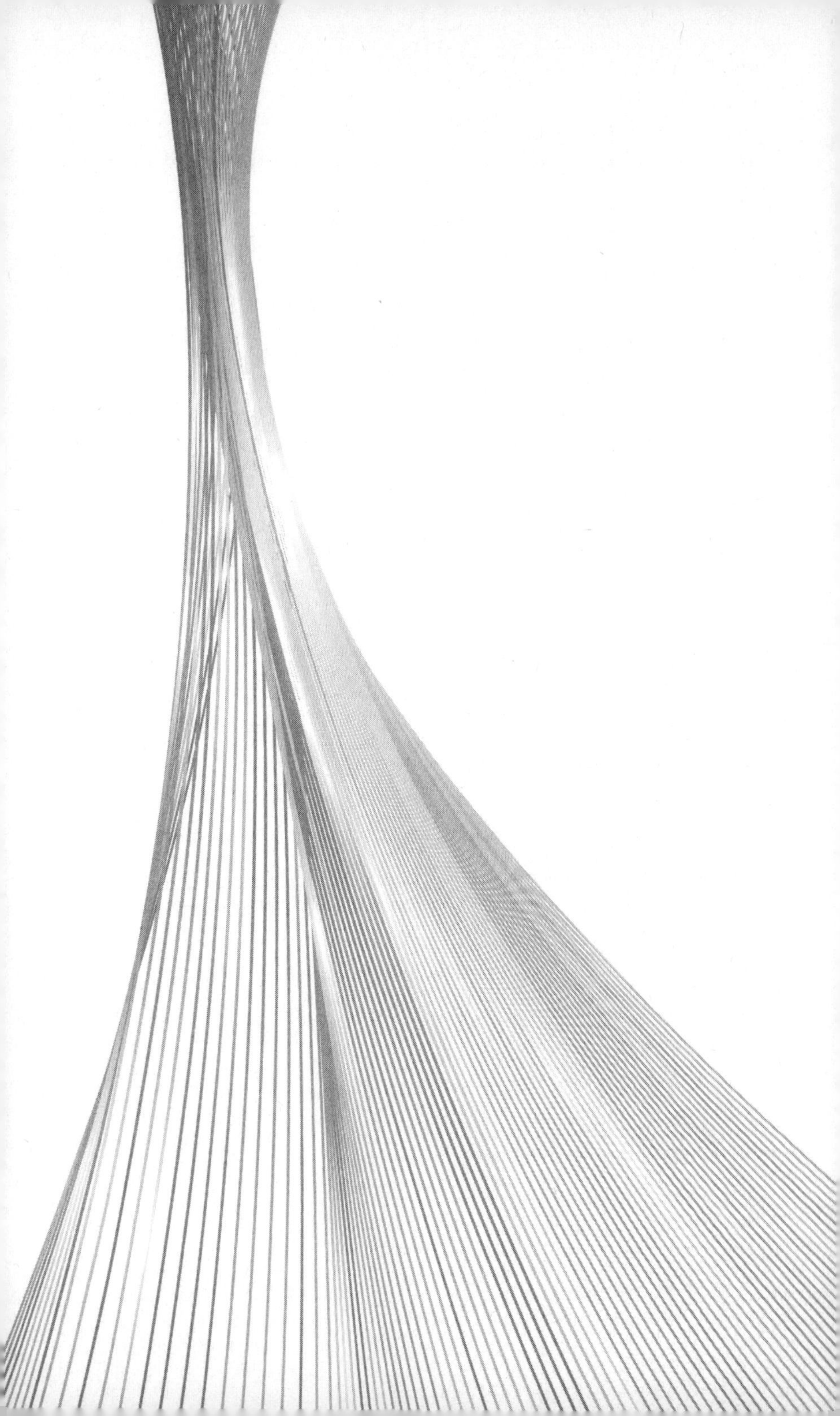

1

The Source of Flow

Having the freedom to choose in any moment to align with the flow of life rather than struggle against it requires us to know a few things. First and foremost, we have to know that the expanded state of consciousness known as flow state actually exists and that we're not restricted to the instinctive reactions of our primitive survival responses, habitual though they may be. To choose flow, we must understand that it is a state of consciousness that exists, just as surely as the survival state exists. It's a wavelength that is available to us in every moment. This includes moments of expansion, ecstasy, and fulfillment, and it also includes moments of pain, desperation, and constriction.

Next, we need to know that we have the capacity to tap into this state of consciousness anytime we choose—that we are, in fact, divinely designed to live in flow and that our human machinery comes equipped with everything needed to operate on these higher, freer, and more fluid planes of awareness.

Finally, we have to know exactly *how* to access this state of being—on purpose and for sustained periods of time, whenever we so desire. We need to understand that elevating into flow state is every bit as accessible to us as spiraling into the survival state of a fight, flight, freeze, or fawn response. In other words, flow state is something that we can choose to generate within ourselves at will, not something that simply "happens" to us from time to time when conditions are just right.

It's my promise to you that this book will explore all three of these points of knowledge in-depth and that, by the end of it, it's my intention that you will become a master at shifting out of survival mode and into flow, at moving out of pain and into pleasure, and at feeling and attracting more of what you do want and less of what you don't want, so you can live your life every day to the fullest. All of this will unfold as we continue through the coming chapters. For now, we're going to start at the beginning by diving into the very first assertion, what you must accept as truth to master the Flow Factor. How can we be sure that the beautiful and rarefied state of being called flow actually exists and is possible to achieve? What is the Flow Factor, exactly, and what is the source of that flow?

The Source of Flow

There are several ways we can approach this understanding. We can drop into it by recalling the wisdom passed down to us from ancient philosophies as diverse as Buddhism, Hinduism, Sufism, shamanism, and Indigenous traditions, which tell us that all of life is funded (or sourced) by an infinite stream of energy and intelligence. This stream is life force itself—the unseen presence that is responsible for the growth of a single human fetus, the expansion of infinite galaxies, and everything in-between.

The Source of Flow

Likewise, we could seek to understand the origins of flow by studying the mind-blowing discoveries of quantum physics, which tell us that everything that appears to our senses as dense physical matter is actually made up of electrons that, when studied closely, amount to nothing more than clouds of empty space. At the basis of everything our senses perceive as separate is one unified field—a vast and connected ocean of awareness. What we call "reality" is nothing but waves that rise and fall in and out of existence, depending on where we choose to focus the powerful energy stream of our attention.

We could also validate the existence of flow by peering through the lens of neurobiology, which has scientifically observed and measured how dramatically our physiology changes when we are in a state of flow versus a survival state of reacting to triggers with the fight, flight, freeze, or fawn responses. And we will do a bit of all of this before our time together comes to a close.

But since I am neither a philosopher nor a physicist nor a neurobiologist, I'm going to explain flow in everyday language: Flow feels good! Flow feels easy and effortless. Being in the flow opens doors and makes us feel that we are provided for and supported. Flow is what naturally occurs when we're in a state of alignment with the field of pure positive, unlimited energy. It's the result of operating in harmony with, rather than in opposition to, the energy stream that created you, me, and every living thing and that sources and sustains worlds.

This energy is who we are at our core; it's what the body, mind, and soul are made of. The source of flow is none other than the very quantum soup that we're all born from, that sustains our body while we're incarnated in it, and that we return to after our body dies. It's the life force energy that enters when we take our first breath and leaves when we have taken our last. Throughout time, this energy has been known by many names. Eastern healing traditions refer to it as life force, *prana*, and infinite intelligence, or chi. Religious traditions refer to it as the many different names for God. By whatever name you call it, it's undisputable that everything in our physical universe is sourced by a flow of nonphysical energy, a highly intelligent, responsive current that keeps our Earth revolving in perfect orbit around the sun and electrons orbiting in harmony around the nucleus of every atom.

Our human nervous system, with its network of sophisticated energy transmitting and receiving centers, is an extension of this universal intelligence. We are designed to operate in perfect communion and connection with the stream of energy that creates worlds, and in our natural and balanced state, this energy flows through us easily, joyfully, and abundantly—like water rushes through an open pipe. *This* is flow state, and when we're in it, we experience balance, ease, gratitude, joy, love, success, and abundance in all its forms. And since the goal of this book is to equip you with a multitude of ways to access this state of consciousness at will, it's worth taking an in-depth look at all the features that are associated with this state of being.

Before we enter this mysterious world of what flow is, it makes sense to first define what flow is not. As I describe for you some of the experiences and characteristics that indicate the absence of flow, I feel certain it will leave you nodding in agreement because the truth is, we have all experienced flow—and its absence—many, many times throughout life.

What Flow Is Not

When flow is absent, we have the experience of pushing hard to achieve an outcome that we believe is necessary for us to be happy, only to realize that the harder we push, the more things don't go our way and the more unhappiness we feel. It seems like nothing we do is ever good enough and the outcomes that we do manage to create come with the heavy price tag of hard work and exhaustion. The opposite of flow is having the experience, perhaps over and over, that we are running up against a near-constant stream of adversity or the sensation of feeling utterly paralyzed by internal resistance even when no external obstacles are present. The absence of flow is characterized by that feeling we've all sunk into from time to time, that the entire universe is working against us—conspiring against us, even—as roadblocks and adversaries to what we desire seem to come out of the woodwork to foil our plans.

The opposite of flow is what you experience after being blessed with a fleeting glimpse of an entirely different slice of reality that you could be living—a version of yourself that is more refined, rarefied, evolved, happy—only to watch that vision collapse like a heavy curtain being pulled across a stage. In fact, one of the most excruciating features of entering flow by chance—in a drug-induced state, for example, or in an environment like a dream vacation where circumstances are incredibly, unrealistically blissful—is that we often stay in this magical state just long enough to envision a more magnificent version of ourselves or the flawless way a particular project could turn out, but then immediately after, instead of seeing the lighted path that will lead us toward that expanded reality, all we see are all the roadblocks in the way.

Where flow state affords us a broader perspective that enables us to see everything and everyone around us as potential opportunities and allies, in survival state, we have tunnel vision, meaning we view everything and everyone as a potential problem or threat. When we're cut off from flow, we perceive ourselves as powerless and incapable, as victims of other people and outside circumstances. We flip-flop between the predictable and repetitive roles within what psychoanalyst Stephen Karpman identified as the Drama

Triangle—that of the Victim, the Persecutor, and the Rescuer—feeling either that we've been wronged, that we're justified in our anger, or that we're saddled with the thankless job of cleaning up everyone else's mess. When we feel trapped in survival mode and utterly without choice, our internal dialogue reflects sentiments such as: *It shouldn't be this hard. There must be something wrong with me. Life isn't fair. It's someone else's fault.* You get the idea.

If an absence of flow is marked by struggle and resistance as we hold ourselves apart from the energy that underlies all things, flow state is accompanied by profound ease as we align with, receive, and become conduits for this powerful energy stream.

So, What Exactly Is the Flow?

There is a flow to all of life—an extremely intelligent, highly responsive current of energy that brings order to all things, sustains all of life, and governs every act of manifestation from the planetary to the individual. The flow of energy that connects us with a loved one, regardless of the distance between us, is the same intelligence that orchestrates the growth of a single microscopic cell into a highly complex human being. Flow is the birthplace of all innovation, all creativity, inspiration, and love. It can be seen as the light in our eyes when we suddenly conceive of a genius solution. It can be felt as the comforting sense of blessedness that comes over us when we find ourselves, often inexplicably, at just the right place at just the right time. Flow is the force that breathes life into every new desire that is born within our hearts, and it's the force that—if we allow it—will nurture those desires into their fullest expression.

Flow is a state of allowance, engagement, and interest, a coexistence of relaxation in the nervous system and alertness in the mind. It's that unmistakable feeling of being on a roll, at the top of your game, and firing on all cylinders. Solutions and opportunities unfold easily, almost magically. In flow, each idea, decision, and action leads seamlessly to the next, and we see potential resources and opportunities in virtually everyone we meet.

When we're in flow, we feel our best and perform our best. Our inner awareness merges with whatever action we're engaged in, we no longer feel bound by time or space, and our individual sense of self dissolves into the greater whole. Flow is that coveted state that athletes refer to as "being in the zone." Yet it would be incomplete to define flow only as a state of peak performance because it's accessible to all of us. The experience of flow is universal, which means it's experienced across all classes, genders, ages, cultures, and physical shapes and sizes and is accessible in all environments and arenas of life—not just in those that are harmonious and abundant.

It doesn't matter where you look—in the world of sports or music, in the field of medicine or business, in the art world or in the art of parenting—in every domain of human experience where you find people who are happy, fulfilled, and experiencing success without struggle, you will find the exact same energetic signature: the genius state of expanded consciousness that researchers refer to as flow.

Survival State versus Flow State

Flow state and survival state exist at opposite poles along the continuum of our consciousness. At one end or extreme, we have our hardwired, animalistic instinct to survive, which locks us into four rudimentary ways of responding in any given situation: *fight, flight, freeze,* or *fawn*. This means, if we're in survival state and something is happening that's other than the outcome we desire, we're compelled to reflexively push against it, make it wrong, or try to bend it to our will (fight). Or we try to avoid it, outrun it, numb ourselves to it, or physically remove ourselves from its influence (flight). In response to the unwanted occurrence, we might become paralyzed into inaction, playing our own human game of "possum," hoping that the contrasting situation will magically go away (freeze). Or we might don the role of the helper, rescuer, or peacekeeper and attempt to sway the outcome in our favor through our charms (fawn).

These four responses are variations of our most primitive survival instincts and represent the basest or lowest level of consciousness that we can experience. Survival state is rooted in a perception of scarcity, limitation, and competition, and we are just as frequently triggered into this state because of past traumas as we are in the presence of a threat happening in the moment. We'll explore more on this in chapter four.

At the opposite end of survival state on the spectrum of consciousness is flow state, an experience that is rooted in faith in the universe and certainty of the abundance of choices that are always available to us. When we're in flow state, we take contrasting events in stride, knowing there is nothing to be gained by working ourselves into a tight ball of resistance to whatever is happening in the moment. Survival state and flow state represent the duality between our humanity and our divinity: our animal desire to contract, cling, and react to life, and our spiritual desire to release, expand, and create.

As long as we are incarnated in a human body, we will never completely transcend our survival response—this is neither possible nor desirable. But what most of us who are living primarily in survival mode don't yet understand is that we were born with the ability to navigate freely through each of these extremes of consciousness; we're not doomed to live in an exhausting and unfulfilling state of fight or flight. In other words, we're designed to shift freely between the two.

In survival state, we actively recoil from life's pain and run toward life's pleasure. Seeking pleasure and avoiding pain is, after all, the purpose of our fight-or-flight instincts. For example, when our body temperature drops, we're hardwired to search for shelter. When we get hungry enough, we hunt for food. But the key difference is this: In survival state, we run from pain as though it's something that can be avoided, whereas in flow state, we recognize pain and pleasure as two sides of the same coin and wisely ride the waves of both, knowing that the one is not possible without the other. We could never know the pleasure or joy of life if we hadn't experienced its pain or deprivation. Nothing would taste as sweet or quench our thirst as deeply if it were not for the presence of hunger or thirst. Having and losing, fullness and emptiness, light and dark, pleasure and pain—these polarities are what make our brief time on life on planet Earth both possible and meaningful.

We came into this human experience with the intention to remember that we would never be able to experience the lower frequencies of life if it were not for the existence of the higher frequencies and vice versa. We came forth intending to remember that our experience of reality is primarily shaped by our perception of it—and therefore, we are always free to move in the direction of flow, even when we're surrounded by unwanted or contrasting circumstances.

The rub, of course, is that it's incredibly easy to lose sight of this inherent freedom when we're knee-deep in the contrast. When we are faced with the very visceral experience that something that really matters to us is slipping away or not turning out the way we deeply desire it to, it is so incredibly easy to lose hours, days, or even years resisting those circumstances. It's easy to give in to thoughts like *Why isn't this manifesting the way I want it when I'm working as hard as I can and giving all I know how to give? I'm already overworked and overwhelmed. I can't do more than I'm already doing. Why is this happening to me?* It's easy to feel defeated by the utter frustration of trying our very best to overcome some troubling situation, only to be faced with the perception that we're powerless over it. It's easy to become discouraged that, despite our best efforts, we still haven't paid off the debt, or met our soulmate, or launched the business, or gotten pregnant. Despite our best efforts, everyone we love will one day die, and everything in this physical world that we treasure will one day turn to dust. Is the experience of flow even possible in a world of such extreme circumstances?

I want you to know that I know the agony of feeling stuck in life's contrast and apart from life's flow because I have been there, more times than I can count. I know how easy it is to continue turning down the well-trodden path of feeling like a victim, or being angry at the universe, or flipping birds in the air in a defiant "Screw it," because we feel there is just no way out. What I also want you to know is that there is always a way out. There is always an instantaneous path from resistance back into flow because this change requires only a shift in our consciousness, not manipulating external conditions to give us a smoother ride.

Flow state is not something we achieve once we finally find a solution to that troubling circumstance—when we receive the news that our health scare was over nothing or when the crisis in our business blows over. Everything—and I mean, *everything*—comes down to the state of our consciousness, and when we feel trapped, it only means that our consciousness is, in that moment at least, residing in the more resistant end of the spectrum. Yet to find ourselves lost in a contrasting experience or temporarily

The Source of Flow

"stuck" in a reaction of fight, flight, freeze, or fawn is not a sign that anything has gone wrong. It's a sign that we are human. We are living the experience we came here to live, venturing into the dark, so to speak, so we can realize more of our light. In response to life's inevitable contrast and pain, we can react instinctively and try only to survive the unpleasantness, or we can wisely and courageously choose to flow our energy despite it. The first choice leads to desperation and a diminishment of our life force. The second, to a sense of personal empowerment and self-mastery, as well as illumination for all who witness it.

Our history books are filled with examples of people who sought and found the experience of flow even in the most extreme of contrasting experiences. One legendary case is that of Mahatma Gandhi, who maintained his devotion to the principle of nonviolence even as he endured oppression, countless arrests, and years-long imprisonment and physical assaults. When asked how he was able to sustain his commitment to peace in the midst of the torturous conditions that surrounded him, Gandhi is said to have replied, "You can chain me, you can torture me, you can even destroy this body, but you will never imprison my mind." Not only was the power of Gandhi's nonviolent protests pivotal in helping India regain freedom after nearly one hundred years of tyranny under British rule, but his work went on to shape the thinking of a generation of civil rights activists to come, including that of Dr. Martin Luther King Jr.

Around this same period and on the other side of the world, Austrian psychiatrist Viktor Frankl spent years imprisoned in Nazi concentration camps, where he endured unimaginable horrors, including witnessing the murder of his mother, father, brother, and countless innocent others. And yet, in the midst of what would have been for most an experience of unthinkable suffering, Frankl maintained that the only freedom that cannot be stripped from a human being is the freedom to "choose one's own attitude in any given set of circumstances, to choose one's own way." In focusing on this freedom and choosing to spend his days providing as much comfort as he could to his fellow prisoners, he found meaning, purpose, joy, and flow. Frankl not only survived the Holocaust but went on to write the renowned book *Man's Search for Meaning*, where the above quote from him originally appeared.

From these extreme cases and many others, it's clear that the experience of flow is not something that's attainable only in a peaceful or adversity-free environment. In fact, it's often only when we are facing truly dire contrast and our most primal survival instincts are triggered that we realize our full capacity for flow. When the stakes are high and everything we love and care about is on the line, the contrast of that experience becomes a powerful catalyst that helps us to defocus on everything unimportant and call into action the skills and abilities from deep within us that we probably never knew we had.

This was certainly the case when my husband and I received the news that our infant son, Maxim, would need a risky open-heart surgery to correct a congenital heart valve problem that was discovered when he was just two months old. Although we were surrounded by the energies of fear, pity, and negativity from hospital staff and family members alike, Frederic and I stayed focused within the flow of the energy that we wanted, which was having our baby boy home in time for Christmas and growing up to be a healthy and happy kid. This is the flow of energy that won out in the end, and I am overcome with gratitude every time I recall this experience. Contrast clarifies within our hearts what is truly important to us and causes us to launch into the universe a powerful "ask" for that desire to be fulfilled. Our task is to then as quickly as possible shift out of survival mode and back into flow so we can receive what we have asked for.

The Source of Flow

The point of sharing these examples is this: You didn't come here looking for perfect conditions so that you could experience the state of flow that is your birthright. You may think you did, but you didn't. You came here to learn how to master your energy so you can find flow under any circumstance or condition. You intended to navigate the magnificent variety of experiences that planet Earth provides with the same skill as a master pianist who uses every note on the keyboard when composing his symphony. You may have been taught that the path to happiness and success is to make yourself strong or crafty enough to outrun life's painful circumstances, but—as I'm sure you have discovered by now—this is an impossible task. The path to both happiness and success lies in harnessing our ability to flow our energy in harmony with the inner experience we desire, regardless of what is happening in the external world.

There is an old saying that life is a teacher to the wise person and an enemy to the fool. I have always taken this to mean that the same energy stream that can give us the experience of exquisite freedom, joy, and flow can also give us the experience of frustration, terror, apathy, or resignation. Source energy is the energy that funds all things, period. When we're cooperating with and in harmony with this stream, we experience flow. When we are working hard to bend the river of life to our will, we instinctively know we're up against an unwinnable battle, and so our survival strategies spring fully into gear. In those moments, the same stream that gives us life-giving inspiration, ideas, and pleasure beats us against the rocks, yielding frustration, exhaustion, and despair. But as you'll discover in the pages that follow, anytime we feel locked into a lower, slower, more resistant state of consciousness, all that is required is for us to turn ourselves in body and mind back into alignment with the stream.

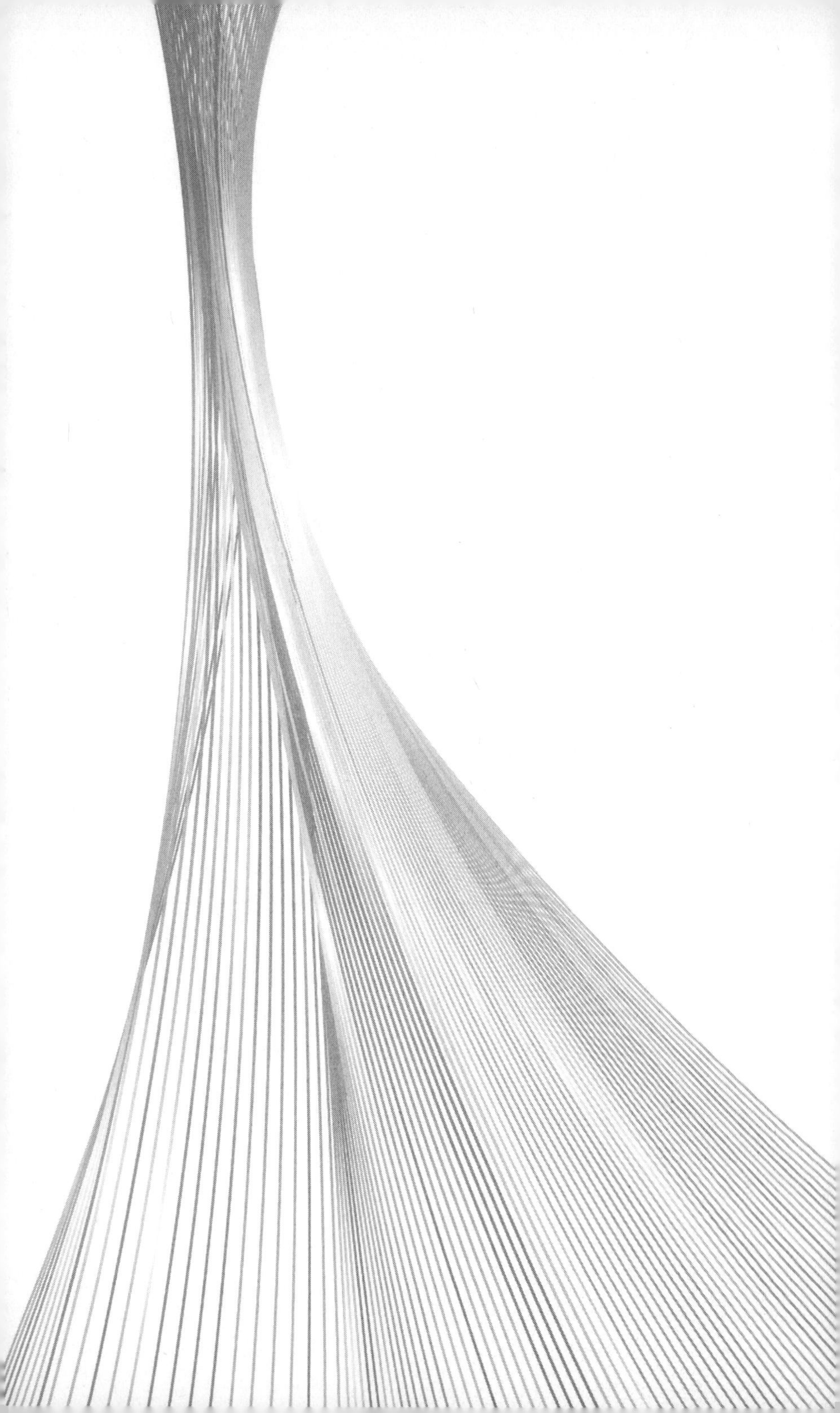

2

Unlocking the Power of Your Free Will

Let's begin this exploration into the power of free will by circling back to a concept I asked you to consider in the first chapter: *Flow state and survival state coexist.*

By coexist, I mean that in every moment, we have the capacity to align our energies with either of these extremes in consciousness—or with any other state of consciousness between. Another way of saying this is, despite how it may appear, there is no condition horrible enough to prevent us from flowing our energies in the direction that we desire, and there is no situation blissful enough to carry us into a state of flow if internally we're balled up in a state of resistance. Your own personal experience has likely already shown this to be true.

For example: Have you ever found yourself in what you had always imagined would be an idyllic moment in time—maybe on an exotic romantic getaway or having earned a reward for some outstanding achievement in your career—but for whatever reason, you were unable to really let in the joy and abundance of the experience? Like, although your body was on the beach with your loved one, your mind was ruminating over the poor service you received at the hotel the night before or taking inventory of all the tasks piling up at home. Or maybe right before your big career win, you heard a piece of office gossip that triggered your defenses, took you out of the present moment, and sent you reeling emotionally. In both examples, the outer conditions were near perfect, but your internal state of resistance was blocking you—in that moment, at least—from moving into the high, celebratory, joyful vibration that is flow.

You've probably also experienced the flip side of this coin—when you were in a stressful, tense, or otherwise undesirable situation, but you found a way to feel good and flow your energy in a positive direction anyway. Maybe you used the trying situation as an opportunity to show yourself that you can, in fact, shine in a crisis, or you may have stopped any potential angst from gaining a foothold by consciously reflecting on all your blessings. Regardless of the strategy you used, you found a way to stay out of the fray and maintain the autonomy of your own high vibration, regardless of what those around you were doing.

If either of these scenarios rings true, then you already know in your heart that the Flow Factor—like the experience of falling in love or being overcome by a fit of genuine belly laughter—is something you must allow yourself to move into from the inside out, and not something that can be asserted into your experience from the outside in. The reason that the switch to both survival mode and flow state can only be flipped from within is because flow state and survival state are not just states of manifestation. They are states of consciousness.

Unlocking the Power of Your Free Will

Now this, in and of itself, is life-changing information. If we were to really understand and embrace this one spiritual truth, we would never again attach our happiness, our success, or our experience of feeling loved, important, and deserving to any external person or thing. The knowledge that we are the ones who allow or deny these experiences from within would free us from the tiresome grind of trying to get people, places, and things to go our way in order for us to feel good. We would know that to move from fear to flow, from despair to happiness, and from panic-inducing scarcity into lavish abundance, absolutely nothing needs to change, except the state of our consciousness.

But here's the thing: The knowledge that a shift in consciousness is all it takes to go from experiencing life as a constant struggle for survival to experiencing it as a continuous flow is not enough to set you completely free. To cash in on the immense influence that your state of consciousness has on your experience of reality, you first must understand what exactly your consciousness is made of and what causes it to fluctuate between the states of constriction and expansion. You also have to know that although external influences will always be a factor in your experience, you are the one with ultimate dominion over your state of consciousness. Most important of all, you need to know that whether your consciousness is flying high on the wavelength of flow or circling the drain in survival mode comes down to the degree to which you have claimed the power of your own free will.

You see, most of us know through our lived experience that our state of consciousness can shift in an instant, but we don't understand exactly why or how this occurs. All we know is one minute we're feeling good and flowing through our day—then something happens that we don't like and suddenly we feel angry or defeated. But the expansion or contraction of our state of consciousness—which is to say, the rise or fall of our mood and our mindset—doesn't happen by accident, and it never happens without our consent. In actuality, we cosign on our departure from flow at every step of our experience, from how we choose to perceive a situation to the actions we take in response to it. By exploring each layer of our operating consciousness, we begin to understand exactly how it is that we allow the resistance to creep in—and gain important insights on what steps we can take to remain in better command of our own energies.

To get to the place we're headed in this chapter—which is for you to know in every cell of your being that flow is a state of consciousness that you have the power to access in any situation—we need to examine the five separate, but highly interrelated, levels of our being that make up our moment-to-moment consciousness, then consider how our own free will can impact our experience at each level.

The Anatomy of Consciousness

The debate over consciousness—what it is, where it comes from, and, in some scientific circles, whether it exists at all—dates back hundreds of years. Today, science, medicine, and philosophy give a common definition of consciousness as "a state of being awake and aware of one's surroundings." In other words, one thing we can say for sure about consciousness is that it encompasses at least our own subjective experience of ourselves and our environment. But then, of course, the question arises: What creates our subjective experience? Why is my subjective experience different from yours? And how is it that even the same person's subjective state of consciousness can vary so dramatically from day to day, even moment by moment?

What you will know for certain by the end of this chapter is this: Your brain function is different in different states of consciousness.

Your perception is different in different states of consciousness. Same with your thoughts and emotions. The words you're compelled to speak and the actions you're compelled to take also vary wildly depending on your state of consciousness. In and of itself, consciousness is a neutral field of awareness, but in the same way that a movie projector can play any genre of film from comedy to horror, your consciousness is capable of supporting an entire range of experiences. In other words, your consciousness is the medium that allows you to transmit, contain, and receive energy, and that which you call reality is simply a function of your state of consciousness.

Conversationally, we refer to our state of consciousness as our frame of mind or headspace, or the wavelength we're vibrating on. From an energetic standpoint, nothing is more important than our moment-to-moment state of consciousness. It's the medium through which we engage with life, the starting point of everything that we create. It's our unique energetic signature—the combination of perspective, thoughts, feelings, words, and actions—to which everything and everyone in this energetic universe registers and responds to.

This is the basic principle of the Law of Attraction, which I'm sure you're familiar with by this point: The energy we send out into the world vibrates in harmony with and returns to us all other like energies. Because of this phenomenon, your level of consciousness is incredibly important. So here, then, are the five interrelated functions that make up the state of our moment-to-moment consciousness.

PERCEPTION

Your perception is the unique vantage point through which you view the world around you. And because you, like nearly everyone, probably believe the adage "seeing is believing," your natural tendency is to assume that the way you perceive reality is an accurate representation of what reality truly is.

It's essential to realize that through the lens of your perception, you are not seeing "reality"—you are only seeing your interpretation of reality. As Stephen Covey wrote in his 1989 classic *The 7 Habits of Highly Effective People*, "We see the world, not as it is, but as we are." Our perception influences who we believe we are, how we believe our interactions with others should go, and how we believe the world should operate. But the lens of our perception is colored by all kinds of things—our moods, our expectations, our past experiences, even physical factors such as being tired or hungry. In other words, when we make an observation about something or someone, that observation leads almost immediately to a conclusion that is based not in truth but in our own personal experience.

A classic example of this phenomenon originates from Vedanta, a Hindu philosophy that teaches that the goal of life is to manifest one's divinity: While walking outdoors at night, a man nearly steps on what looks like a dangerous snake, coiled and ready to strike. Terrified, he quickly runs away. In the light of the next day, he returns to that same spot and realizes that what he perceived to be a snake was only a rope. Like the man who mistook the rope for a snake, our perceptions are often formed through ignorance or incorrect conclusions, yet we respond to them as if they are the truth.

So, we view every piece of data that comes our way through our own personal lens, and then—in the privacy of our own hearts and minds—we alone decide if it is an opportunity or a threat, if it's a reason to celebrate in delight, to lash out at in defense, or to slink away from in fear. As Oprah Winfrey and Bruce Perry explained in their 2021 bestseller, *What Happened to You?*, "The brain is a meaning-making machine, always trying to make sense of the world. If our view of the world is that people are good, then we will anticipate good things." Ultimately, it is our perception of an experience that creates our feelings about it, not the event itself.

Years ago, I heard a Taoist teaching story from the *Huainanzi*, a collection of Chinese philosophical essays dating back to the second century BCE, that expresses this understanding beautifully. The story goes that there was once a Chinese farmer whose best horse ran away. On hearing this, the man's neighbors sought him out to express their condolences. "We are sorry to hear of this bad news," they said. As the story goes, the farmer only shrugged and said, "Good news, bad news. Who can say?" Soon after, the farmer's horse returned to the stable with three wild horses in tow, substantially increasing the farmer's bounty. Again, his neighbors approached, congratulating him on this fortunate turn of events. And again, the farmer shrugged and replied only, "Good news, bad news. Who can say?" The father gave the strongest of the new horses to his adult son, but the moment his son tried to ride it, the animal raised up violently and threw the younger man to the ground, breaking his leg. "Such bad news," his neighbors tutted in sympathy. "Good news, bad news. Who can say?" was the farmer's only response. In the week that followed, the emperor's soldiers entered the farmer's village to round up all the able-bodied young men to fight in a distant war, but because of his broken leg, the farmer's son was spared from the draft. The neighbors once again congratulated the farmer upon hearing this "good news," and the farmer, as you might have guessed, simply shrugged, understanding that good news and bad news are byproducts of our perception, nothing more.

If, instead of launching immediately into a conclusion or responding with a positive or negative judgment about events, we could do as the farmer did and linger in pure observation in the realm of *Who knows?* or *How interesting?*, we could spare ourselves the roller-coaster ride of reacting to our own conclusions and leave ourselves a little more open to perceiving the divine flow in all things.

There is no one meaning that can be assigned to any event in life. Rather, it's our perception and interpretation of life's events that dictate how we feel about them. The same external event that causes us to coil up in fear or anger could just as easily cause our hearts to burst open in joy and gratitude. This is the incredible power of our free will: Whether we declare something as good news or as bad news, we are right.

THOUGHTS

How we perceive a thing naturally gives rise to the thoughts we think about it. Perceive it as an opportunity, and your mind will flood you with creative and imaginative thoughts about what's possible, what solutions may come of it, and the enjoyment you might experience as a result of engaging with it. Perceive it as a threat, and violà—you discover that your mind has an equal capacity for suspicion, catastrophizing, and fabricating emergencies, problems, and worst-case scenarios where none may actually exist. To activate the power of the Flow Factor, you—the energetic being inhabiting a body—need to take ownership of the mind rather than blindly taking orders from it.

The thoughts we think generate a stream of energy, and this stream carries us in one of two directions: Our thoughts are either affirming our blessings, lifting us up, and opening our eyes to new possibilities and pathways to experience flow, or they are painting us into a corner, bringing us down, and pointing out every obstacle—real and very much imagined—that stands in our way of flow. In other words, our thoughts matter, a lot. We cannot think thoughts that hurt our hearts, deflate our energy, cause our fists to clench in rage, or our stomachs to turn over in knots, and simultaneously allow the energy of the universe to unfold its blessings to us.

Think of your brain like the rideshare driver who shows up in response to your request with a fueled-up car and a GPS device that is ready to take you to whatever address you provide. Now imagine asking that driver to program their GPS with one of these undesirable destinations:

- *I don't do well with change.*

- *I shy away from intimacy.*

- *It's hard for me to ask for what I want.*

- *I never meet anyone interesting.*

- *In my family, I have to be the peacekeeper.*

- *My business is bleeding money.*

- *It's too late for me to start again.*

- *I suck at relationships.*

Wow, right?! From this example, you can see how once the momentum of a particular train of thought gets rolling, it can carry us pretty quickly to an unwanted destination—just as surely as your driver will take you to whatever address you provide, whether it's a palace or a shack. The universal principle at work here is, *You get what you think about, whether it is something you want or something that you don't want.* Or, as my friend John Assaraf recently shared during the Moving Beyond Contrast Summit that I led: "Most people are thinking about what they don't want, then wondering why it shows up over and over again."

The power that the mind holds in shaping our reality is a central tenet of Buddhist philosophy, dating back thousands of years. The actual quote from the *Dhammapada*, a collection of sayings and verses from the early Buddhist tradition, goes like this: "If a man speak or act with an evil thought, suffering follows him as the wheel follows the hoof of the beast that draws the wagon. . . . If a man speak or act with a good thought, happiness follows him like a shadow that never leaves him." In other words, our thoughts matter—a lot!

So, if you think it's a dog-eat-dog world, it is one, and you'd better hang out in survival mode to keep the pack from eating you. If you think it takes back-breaking effort to be successful, it will, so you'd better keep on grinding. And if you think that flow is your natural state that's always accessible, you won't routinely offer thoughts of resistance, so you'll get there easily.

We are the only ones who can choose the direction of our thoughts. We are the only ones who can choose to entertain thoughts that feel bad or to reach for thoughts that feel better. There is such incredible, powerful, free will in the human mind. It is not bound to a physical body, and it's restricted by nothing. In a split second, it can travel anywhere in the known or unknown universe and entertain any notion, from contemplating the tiniest grain of sand to the infinity of this galaxy and all those beyond it. As the navigator of the engine that is our brain, it's up to us to steer it in the direction of flow rather than fear. Rather than automatically climbing aboard any old train of thought that comes our way, we can engage our free will to make sure we're actually interested in arriving at the destination it's pointing us toward.

FEELINGS

Just as our perceptions influence our thoughts, our thoughts influence our feelings. The connection between the two is supported by extensive research in the fields of both psychology and neuroscience. Milliseconds after you think a thought, that thought will generate a corresponding feeling within you. For example, thinking about a dog might generate a feeling of fear or a feeling of excitement, depending on what you hold to be true about dogs. Another way of saying this is that a feeling is a physical manifestation of a thought. The important thing to understand is that by the time you're feeling something, your perceptions and thoughts have already become a manifested part of your biology. Your heart races with anxiety, your breathing deepens with anticipation, you have become physically affected by that thought. Compared to our perceptions and thoughts, feelings provide even more tangible evidence of our state of consciousness. We feel great when we're in flow, and we feel some version of lousy when we're in survival mode.

Now, to be fair, feelings really do have a way of catching a person off guard. You can be humming along, in the flow, noticing the beauty around you and basking in all manner of high-frequency thoughts—and something or someone can enter your experience that triggers an unpleasant emotion within you that seems to come out of the blue: A song comes on the radio that you played on repeat during a really low point in your life. A woman walks across the street wearing a scarf just like your mom used to wear. You pass by a bakery, and the scent takes you back, wistfully, to the time you were in Italy with the person you thought was the great love of your life . . . and suddenly, splat. Your vibration crashes like a wave against a seawall and you're left with a heavy, resistant feeling where moments before you were feeling lighthearted and free.

I call experiences like these *bushwhacks*, a term I picked up from Barbara Brown, a holistic health expert and author I met a few years back while filming a documentary series. The show featured a group of transformational leaders whom the producers would place in a variety of stressful situations to observe how we might react and what tools we would use to settle ourselves back down. When we were informed of a last-minute change to our sleeping arrangements that left us all feeling a bit uneasy, Barbara, in her slow Southern drawl, announced, "Well, that was one hell of a bushwhack." It stuck.

I really like this word, both because it lightens up the seriousness that we often feel when one of our past traumas (big or little) gets reactivated and because it perfectly describes our visceral experience when this happens. Just like a machete can cut down a thick stalk in an instant, bushwhacks can take us in one fell swoop out of flow and into survival mode. Yet even when we get blindsided by circumstances that are completely out of our control, we still have the power to decide how we relate to those circumstances.

You can start by reminding yourself that this feeling didn't come out of nowhere—rather, it was a direct result of your perception and your thoughts about that perception. When you address the cause, you will naturally yield a different effect. For example, is the stack of files on your desk a sign of how overworked you are, or is it a source of livelihood and abundance? Is the empty nest you're now experiencing a harbinger of loneliness and isolation, or is it the first opportunity you've had in decades to get to know and express yourself purely on your own terms? Is the social event you're dreading a burden on your time, or is it a chance to meet and connect with people who could become lifelong friends? Rather than try to push away any unpleasant feelings triggered by your thoughts, you can breathe into the sensation of the emotion and welcome it. Then, if you so desire, you can actively reach into your memory, your imagination, or a completely unrelated topic, to pluck from the buffet of the universe a point of view or a thought that feels better and lighter. You can use your free will to physically take actions that promote a good mood, such as moving your body, going into a different room or location, soaking in a hot bath, laughing, having sex, breathing in the fresh air, or enjoying a few moments in nature. All of these will help jiggle loose your feelings from the perceptions and thoughts that gave rise to them and help you realize that you really do have choice in the matter of how you feel.

So-called negative feelings are simply representative of energy that is moving at a lower, slower frequency because it is running into some sort of resistance (your energetic patterns and emotional triggers). So, you can thank your feelings for letting you know how high and fast—or how low and slow—your level of consciousness is in that moment. Then just be easy about it. It's only energy. Energy is never fixed or permanent; it's always on the move and in the process of changing into a different form.

WORDS

So, you perceive "reality" in a certain light, which then gives you access to a particular bank of thoughts, which then triggers a feeling in your body. The next opportunity you have to exercise your free will is to choose how—or if—you will use words to articulate your current level of consciousness.

I am constantly amazed by the power of words: A simple phrase or story can blow open doors in our mind, lift us into new ways of thinking, and transport us instantly from a mindset of limitation into a new possibility. Of course, words are double-edged swords that can also be used to shred our self-esteem, dash our hopes, send countries into war, and inflict deep wounds among loved ones and friends. With every idea we form into words, we are speaking into existence one of two realities: We're creating either a reality we desire or a reality we dread. We cannot habitually speak about being broke and simultaneously create prosperity. We can't complain about how flawed or unlovable we feel and magnetize the person of our dreams. We can't criticize everything that's wrong about a given situation and simultaneously conceive its solution. As Florence Scovel Shinn, an unsung spiritual teacher who was way ahead of her time, wrote in her book *Your Word Is Your Wand*, published way back in 1928, "The words you speak create your own destiny."

Unlike our perceptions, thoughts, and feelings, which generally speaking stay within the membrane of our inner world, words spring forth and out into the universe, where they gather even more strength and momentum. Once we put our energy into words, we have the very real potential to shift the consciousness of all who are in earshot of what we speak. If you've ever witnessed someone launch into a particularly juicy piece of gossip and seen how others eagerly join in, like a group of sharks at feeding time, you already know that words are powerful, and they are contagious. Here's the thing about words: They don't just describe reality; they create reality. The words we speak are never neutral because we are literally speaking into existence whatever reality we are in the process of describing.

Pay attention to how most people speak, and you'll notice just how often we use our words unconsciously, without any acknowledgment or respect for their creative potency. We say things like "Life is hard," or "Nothing ever works out for me," or "I'm no good at relationships." Without even realizing it, we are speaking into existence a reality that we have no desire to live. When you change the way you speak about yourself and your life, you change the reality you are creating.

I invite you to make the commitment right now to never again speak in contradiction about anything that you desire to create, just as you would never use your words to criticize or speak ill of a beloved child. The following relevant quote is often attributed to film actor and martial arts master Bruce Lee: "Don't speak negatively about yourself, even as a joke. Your body doesn't know the difference. Words are energy and they cast spells, that's why it's called spelling. Change the way you speak about yourself, and you can change your life." This is excellent advice. You can also visit watchyourwords.com, a website I created several years ago, to connect with me and a community of others who are committed to using their words intentionally to raise their vibration and transform their reality. Use your free will and apply the creative power of your words only to those realities you desire to nourish and expand.

ACTIONS

By now you're probably beginning to see exactly how consciousness becomes reality, right? You perceive, then you justify and enhance your perception with thoughts, then you embody those thoughts with feelings. By this time, your internal vibration has gathered so much intensity and momentum that you feel highly compelled to use your words to describe that reality in detail, giving it further color, texture, and dimension. Now, because you are not simply an energetic being but a magnificent three-dimensional being with a body, the impulse naturally arises to act on the reality you have just created inside of you. Action is energy made tangible. Once again, the external actions we take can always be correlated to our internal state of consciousness.

This helps us understand so much! It helps us to recognize that when someone acts out, seemingly irrationally—lashing out in what feels like unjust anger, or breaking down in sadness because they've taken something we've said or done personally, or ghosting us altogether because fleeing felt like their only viable option—their actions are not necessarily a reflection of us. They reflect what's happening in that person's inner world.

Understanding the energy that drives us to action can also help us make sense of our own contradictory behavior: Why we spend hours mindlessly scrolling social media despite our commitment to be more focused and productive. Why we clam up rather than express our needs and desires with our partner, when what we want is a thriving relationship with them. Why we haul off and do something rash—quit our jobs, sell the house, break off the relationship—then wake up out of our trance and wonder what the hell we were thinking.

In moments like these, our primitive survival instincts constrict our vision, shrinking our ability to recognize all the other options that are also within our reach. Anytime we feel overstimulated, stressed out, destabilized, taken advantage of—when we're wound up and feel like a bundle of raw nerves—taking an impulsive action or habitually reaching for a slice of chocolate cake or a fishbowl-size serving of wine, seems like the perfect answer to our problems. We feel cornered, and so fighting, fleeing, freezing, or fawning our way out seems like the only logical next step. If, in moments like these, we could find the wherewithal to expand our focus, we would see just how many other options are available to us. Let me give you a quick example that occurred in my experience recently.

Thanks to the insights and processes shared throughout this book, I have manifested my ideal living space many, many times in my life. Most recently, my family and I moved into my ultimate dream house on a pristine piece of land up in the mountains overlooking the high desert with gorgeous views of plants, animals, and nature out of every one of its many windows. Ours was one of the first homes to be completed in this brand-new community, but it was not the last. One neighbor finished building the house right next door to us just a few months after we were settled, and when they completed their landscaping, it prominently featured a huge and what I considered hideous cactus right in their front yard, in full view from our house.

Well, needless to say, because I am human, my first reaction to this eyesore was not to think, *Hey, live and let live!* and to move easily into a state of flow. Rather, I recoiled in resistance to the presence of this little-t trauma—insignificant though it may seem—and acted out all the stages of creating an unwanted reality that I've been describing for you here. Fortunately, I let myself move down that unpleasant path for only a couple of hours before remembering that I have free will and deciding to practice the Flow Factor process.

I began at the level of my perception to objectively observe my "reality." Because my survival instincts were triggered, my perception had been hyper-focused on this thing that was, in my eyes, an atrocity and a complete blight on an otherwise beautiful landscape. Because this was my perception, my thoughts then offered me valuable nuggets of wisdom (not), such as "This monstrosity has completely ruined our neighborhood," and "I am going to have to look at this thing every day for the rest of my life." In response to those thoughts, I then vacillated between feeling hopeless, angry, sad, and even vindictive. In fact, if I had allowed that initial momentum of energy to manifest into a physical action, I might have felt inspired to yell at the neighbor, move out of the neighborhood, or chop the damn thing down altogether. None of this is super helpful so far, right?

Instead, just like I've been suggesting you do, I took a deep breath and began considering different ways that I might choose to look at this newest addition to my high desert landscape. Almost instantly, because I asked and was willing to receive, I saw that I did have quite a few options.

I thought about a dear friend, who is a feng shui master, and imagined what energetic cures she might offer to de-emphasize the visual impact of my new prickly friend. Next, I thought of going over to the neighbors' house, introducing myself, and asking them if they wouldn't mind planting a different tree, which I would be happy to pay for. As little as thirty seconds into this process, I began to feel some relief as I entertained some new possibilities and consciously put some distance between myself and my so-called problem. At this point, my mind began working in the direction of my desire, rather than in opposition to it. Sure enough, the next thought I had felt even better than the previous two: I could plant my own tree right in front of the neighbor's house, which would block their cactus from my view when I looked out the window.

Now, in light of all these different options, I was feeling spacious and free rather than victimized, angry, and trapped. I then comforted myself further by reminding myself that this cactus represents contrast itself—that every experience in life contains aspects that are both wanted and unwanted—and I began to shift my point of focus to notice and appreciate the many, many things about our neighborhood that are so perfect and delicious. The mountain landscape, the abundance of plants and animals, the silence alternating with the sound of wind in the trees, the infinity of stars at night.

Unlocking the Power of Your Free Will

There is simply so much to appreciate that, in deliberately contemplating it all, I distanced myself completely from my previous viewpoint that centered on that cactus.

So, getting back to the topic of action and the subject of this cactus, I haven't yet taken any. Because I shifted my consciousness about it, it no longer bothers me every time I look at it, and I no longer feel compelled to do something rash. In fact, most times I don't even notice it, but when I do, the sight of it empowers me because it reminds me of how good I am at mastering my own energy. Now this isn't to say that I won't take action at some point in the future, but if and when I do, it won't be an impulsive or disconnected action that will likely only make my situation worse. It will be inspired by flow and will therefore contain all the genius, creativity, good timing, and win-win potentiality that the universe is capable of yielding.

Just in case you're thinking that my upset around the cactus is too trivial an example to be used as a teaching point, I want to suggest that we human beings allow ourselves to get knocked off balance and pulled out of the flow by far less than an undesirable plant obstructing our view. Regardless of age, gender, ethnicity, or socioeconomic status, we all encounter everyday annoyances: forgetting where you placed your phone or keys when you're rushing to get out the door, encountering a longer-than-usual wait at your go-to lunch spot, spilling something on your blouse moments before a meeting, or dealing with slow internet while you're eagerly waiting for something to download.

The point is that in any situation, no matter how big or small the contrast may be, we always have the power to exercise our free will at the level of our perceptions, thoughts, feelings, words, and actions to bring ourselves back into the flow. If we stubbornly stay focused on the contrast and we start listing out all the ways that we are displeased, we only add to our resistance and our displeasure.

By focusing on what feels good and what our options are, we can move out of the energy of the contrast and resistance and back into the energy of flow. And you know what? Even if we lose our minds—which of course we will do from time to time because we're human—and do act from a state of fear or misalignment, no worries. The universe will reflect our state of consciousness back to us, and once again we will have an opportunity to perceive, think, feel, speak, and act more deliberately—to allow the stream of life rather than to resist it.

Are You Allowing or Resisting the Stream?

As we've already discussed, there is only one stream of energy in the universe, but because we are designed with the power of free will, we have the ability to tap into this stream, to resonate and harmonize with it and allow ourselves to move in the direction it's going—or to resist it. It really is that simple.

When we're tapped into and allowing the stream of universal energy to flow to us and through us, that's when we have the most exalted and beautiful experiences possible on the human plane. Flashes of insight, brilliant inventions, sudden answers to problems we've been grappling with for years, glimpsing a new possibility for our lives, falling in love…all of these amazing experiences of flow are the direct result of being tapped into and aligned with the divine energy stream because in our state of nonresistance, we are open and receptive to the full download of its intelligence.

In a state of allowance, our vibration is pure, uncluttered, and unobstructed. We have clarity. We move through the world feeling like we're sailing with the wind at our back, and we yield results that are hundreds of times more effective than anything we can offer from a state of misalignment. When we choose to align with the stream, we are living the life we truly came here to live—as energy masters, using the Flow Factor to our fullest advantage. When we allow resistance or contradiction into any of the aspects of our being that make up our consciousness—our perspectives, thoughts, feelings, words, or actions—our vibrational signal is no longer pure and uncluttered. Our own resistance splits our energies, which means that part of our consciousness is summoning energy toward what we desire, while the other part is diluting our focus by considering all the obstacles to achieving it. It's a sure sign that you have split energy when you find yourself pouring your precious creative energy into contemplating an outcome that you have no desire to create—when you say things like, "I better not blow this presentation," or think silently, *I hope my wife won't be angry with me for leaving dishes in the sink.* Ironically, when your energy is split rather than aligned, you are far more likely to create the very experiences that you were hoping to avoid. When your own consciousness is not clear, those around you seem to amplify and add to that lack of clarity.

Split energy clouds our thinking, clutters our vibration, and introduces unnecessary and unpleasant chaos into our experience. We feel blocked and ineffective, even when no external obstacle exists in our path. This perfectly describes the agonizing experience we've all had of "being in our own way." Contradicted or split energy dilutes our creative power, which is why taking a moment to align ourselves internally before engaging is always a good idea. Consciousness precedes manifestation, which means that nothing is more important to any result than our energetic alignment.

I'm sure you've witnessed the kind of results that unfold when you enter a situation in a state of consciousness that is high-minded and clear. When you interact with any facet of your life feeling whole, complete, empowered, and connected to your purpose with clarity of intention, you have probably seen how people and circumstances seem to fall effortlessly in line with your clarity and intention. Your own connection to the energy that orchestrates all things makes you unstoppable. If obstacles do arise in your path, you instantly see how to avoid or disarm them, or else you don't even notice them at all. The momentum of your clear, connected, and allowing energy stream is simply moving at too fast a clip, so everything within your sphere gets swept along in its current. When you invest your energy into thinking about, imagining, and feeling into the results you want to create and how you desire to feel as you are creating it, your desired experience has a way of unfolding, even if it's not through the exact path that you had envisioned.

I am asking you to remember these lived experiences, because I want to call your attention to the fact that you already have a visceral understanding of how your state of consciousness creates your reality. You have been living the results of this truth your entire life. We are now simply putting words to what you have already discovered to be true as the result of your own life experience. When you walk into any situation in a resistant and defensive state, reacting with fight, flight, freeze, or fawn, you perceive and attract a whole different range of experiences than you would perceive and attract from an expanded state of connection, intuition, and flow.

This brings us full circle to the idea that I asked you to meditate on at the opening of this chapter: The states of flow and survival coexist. Both are available to us at every moment, and each one yields an entirely different set of results in terms of what we manifest in day-to-day life. However—and this is a big however—in addition to coexisting, flow state and survival state are also mutually exclusive. This means we have to withdraw our attention from one in order to experience the other, in the same way we forego one possible destination by making the decision to turn right instead of left at a fork in the road.

What, then, is the mechanism that allows us to choose? If flow state naturally unfolds when our consciousness is high, expanded, and allowing, and survival state is what we experience when we're vibrating in resistance, then how can we invite the energy of flow into those moments where everything in us is screaming out for us to fight, freeze, flight, or fawn? Or, even more to the point, once we realize that we're caught in a fearful, scarce, or powerless state of consciousness—like I was for one afternoon in relation to that darn cactus—what is the path back to empowerment, abundance, ease, and flow? This is the power of free will.

It comes down to this: You believe that flow is something that just magically unfolds—either because conditions are just so or you happen to have been born under a lucky star—or you accept that flow is a state of consciousness, just like fear, scarcity, and insecurity are states of consciousness. If you accept that flow is a state of consciousness, and that your consciousness is under the domain of your free will, you must then accept that you have the power to tap into flow whenever you desire.

Flow state is the result of allowing the stream of energy that creates all things, and survival state is the result of disallowing or resisting it. Period. Full stop. And because you are born with free will, the choice of whether to fight, flight, freeze, fawn, or flow is yours, in every moment of every day. Even in those situations where you are sure you have no choice.

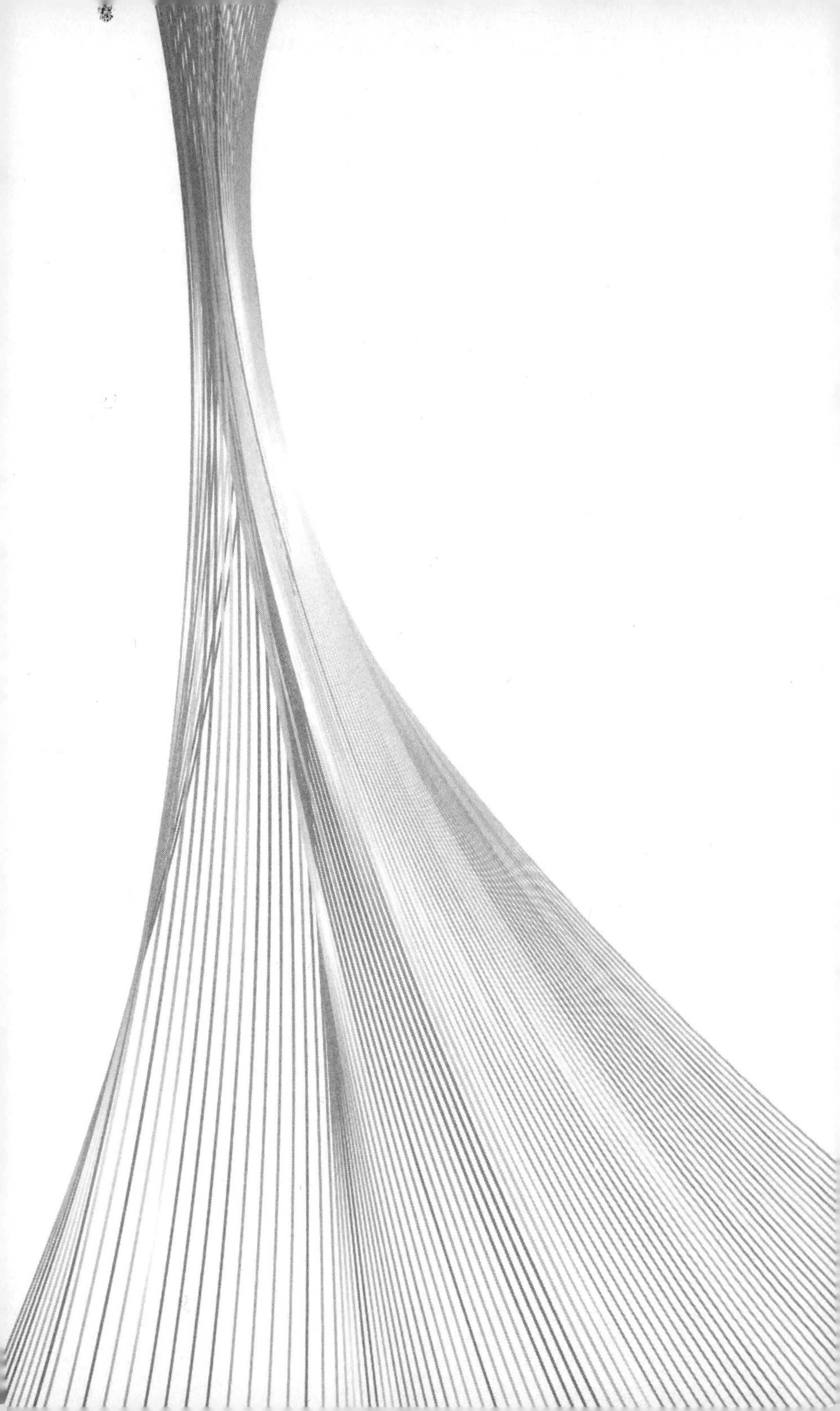

3

Faces of Resistance: Fight, Flight, Freeze, and Fawn

So, the question naturally arises: If it's true (and it is!) that we're all born with the free will to choose between an allowing, joyful state of flow and a pinched-off, resistant state of survival, then why does it so often seem like we have no control over our own mental and emotional states? Why do we sometimes feel like a puppet on a string, a slave to our most primal and unconscious reactions? How is it that we can find ourselves minutes, hours, or even years into a no-good, very bad mood—pessimistic, miserable, and totally out of the flow—with no clue as to how we got there? And why is it that we can be flying high and feeling great, only to suddenly plummet and feel unexpectedly irritated, frustrated or sad?

Remember that this is a book about how to master your energy—which is to say, it's a book about flowing with the pure positive energy that underlies all things rather than harboring an energy of resistance to that flow, at any level of our consciousness. In this chapter, I explore with you some of the ways that you may be holding yourself apart from the flow of energy that you most want to see flourish in your life. Once you can recognize your primal survival reactions simply as temporary manifestations of resistant energy within you, it will become much easier to soften that resistance and move back into flow.

In this chapter, we're going to take a deep dive into the automatic, knee-jerk reactions that keep us in a state of resisting or blocking the very abundance and well-being we desire. Because, like air to birds and water to fish, these habitual reactions can become so much a part of who we are that we don't even realize we're in the throes of them until well after the adrenaline has subsided.

Understanding Our Primitive Survival Reactions

As you already understand, we human beings are born of and from Source energy; we are divine in every way. We're also each born into a physical body that is governed by primitive animal survival instincts. The two parts of our human nervous system reflect these two distinct aspects.

Our limbic system is our brain's threat detection and response center. As defined in the Cleveland Clinic's online health library, "The limbic system is one of the oldest structures of your brain. It produces natural instincts that your ancestors used to survive by triggering behaviors needed to: eat and drink, reproduce, care for young, and react to surroundings (the fight or flight response)." I like to think of it as the watchdog part of our brains.

The limbic system's job is to stay constantly alert to any possible threat to our survival and, if one is detected, to launch the most efficient possible survival mechanism to keep us safe. Just to clarify, by survival, I'm speaking not only of our physical security but also of our emotional, financial, and social well-being. Unlike our ancestors, who fought off saber-tooth tigers in the regular course of earning a livelihood, the "threats" we encounter in our modern world are more subtle but can be every bit as alarming.

This instinctual part of our brain is constantly scanning each person and situation we encounter and asking, *Is this a source of opportunity or danger? Should I befriend or avoid this person? Do I have enough money to buy the groceries and medications I need this month? Am I an accepted and valued part of my community?* Then, anytime we find ourselves faced with a person or situation that feels too overpowering, unpredictable, or chaotic to handle, our limbic system sounds an internal alarm, signaling for us to shift into fight, flight, freeze, or fawn mode to protect ourselves from harm. We've touched on these survival instincts previously, but let's take an in-depth look at each of these four basic mechanisms so you can see how they typically manifest in our day-to-day lives.

The Fight Response

In the presence of a real or perceived threat (and remember, we encounter a perceived threat every time we mistake the proverbial rope for a snake!), our body's fight response prepares us to go to battle, both literally and figuratively. In fight mode, we have the urge to attack a threatening person or situation head-on and are likely to confront the threat and use aggressive behavior, verbal accusations,

The Flow Factor

or even physical force to protect ourselves or what we believe is ours. When our fight instinct is engaged, we can become pushy and overly aggressive in our attempt to either protect ourselves or convince other people that our way of doing and seeing things is the "right" way, and, as maybe you've noticed, they don't even have to be in our vicinity—we could be fighting with others just in the privacy of our own minds. How many times have you caught yourself engaged in a full-blown mental or emotional battle with someone or something that is not even happening in present time? Rather than going with the flow when confronted by one of life's inevitable hiccups, our fight instinct puts us on the offensive and makes us experts at pointing out the flaws of any given person or situation. As the following story illustrates, we can become fully locked and loaded into "fight" mode without ever raising our voice.

On my most recent birthday, my family and I treated ourselves to a lavish trip to Disneyland to celebrate. And right in the middle of the limited window of time when the four of us were given priority access to all the rides, my husband announced that he couldn't find his cell phone. It was a perfect situation for my primal fight instinct to become engaged: It was a special day, I had a strong desire for things to turn out well—it involved an investment of money, and it all needed to occur within a limited window of time. As Frederic continued to search his pockets and reiterated his predicament, I took a deep breath and observed my limbic system powerfully attempting to shift me into battle mode. My pulse quickened, blood rushed to my limbs, and I could feel my inner Alpha Bitch grabbing for the wheel of my consciousness. I had to breathe through the strong impulse to criticize him in front of our kids.

Of course, in a matter of minutes, Frederic had retrieved his phone from where he'd left it using the Find My iPhone app, and luckily, I had enough energy mastery tools in my bag of tricks to

Faces of Resistance: Fight, Flight, Freeze, and Fawn

bring myself back into flow in about the same amount of time. In the end, we all enjoyed the day, and the "lost phone" scenario was just a blip in an overall amazing experience. The point I want to make in sharing this is just how quickly we can go from relaxed and chill into full-scale combat mode. When our fight instinct is engaged, we stop seeing all the points of harmony between ourselves and another and start preparing for battle—even when that battle is with someone we love dearly and are committed to creating a beautiful experience with, and even when that battle is with ourselves or with the universe at large.

Our fight instinct, when reacting to the non-life-threatening circumstances, has us believe that being right is the ultimate victory and urges us to prove that we're right even when it costs us ease, connection, or happiness. It causes us to push others and ourselves relentlessly, and it leaves absolutely no room for the Flow Factor because it holds us in an inflexible stance toward life's unavoidable contrast. As we've already discussed, to be in flow means to continually move with, rather than pit ourselves against, the changes and challenges that are an inevitable part of life, in the same way a skilled surfer adjusts and adapts to the ocean's shifting tides. But when we're in fight mode, we do not adjust or adapt to change. We hold rigidly to what we believe should be happening, and as a result, we completely miss the options and solutions that may be right in front of us, making life much harder for ourselves than it needs to be.

Fight mode denies us the deep peace of surrendering into the present moment, of feeling the serenity that comes from accepting the things we cannot change. It urges us to continue to push up against the problem instead of allowing ourselves to relax and flow more easily into the solution. Rather than being here and now and moving with the current of whatever is happening in this moment, our attention darts between the past and the future. We're either consumed with what might happen in the future if we don't slay whatever dragon we perceive as being presently in our way or we're preoccupied with the injustice of what's happened in the past.

For example, during that lost cell phone episode at Disneyland, my mind immediately flashed back to a family trip we had taken to Australia when the boys were very young. Exhausted and cranky from the eighteen-hour flight, we deboarded the plane, collected our luggage, and were waiting in the baggage area for a driver to take us to our hotel when Frederic realized that he'd left his laptop charger in the seat pocket in front of him on the plane. I told him not to worry about it, that we'd simply buy a new charger the next day, but he insisted on backtracking through the airport in the hopes that he could re-board the plane and retrieve the charger. By the time Frederic returned from this mission, empty-handed, our driver had already come and gone—without us. As this scene unfolded, I launched into fight mode. All my gratitude for our safe arrival into this beautiful place faded to the periphery of my awareness as I dug in my heels in resistance to this one detail of our circumstances.

This is exactly what fight mode does. It keeps us from being fully present where we are, which means it keeps us out of flow, which is a state of being deeply engaged with, and allowing of, the now. The Disneyland event had triggered my memory of this earlier event, and so, mentally, emotionally, and energetically, I was gone—no longer in the present moment and no longer in a state of flow but absorbed in my own exhausting internal struggle against what was happening.

This is why, at some point in the midst of fight mode against those daily moments of inconvenience and perceived threats against not our life but our livelihood, we realize that no amount of defiance will overcome the contrast we're facing, and we unconsciously search for other modes of being that will help us adapt and survive. In an instant we can shift from wanting to fight the situation to wanting to flee instead. Internally we conclude, *I can't take this anymore. I'm out of here.*

The Flight Response

Whereas the fight response prepares us to do battle with anything we perceive as potentially threatening, the flight response urges us to avoid that person or situation at all costs to protect ourselves.

The flight response can show up as calling out sick at work, canceling plans at the last minute, avoiding important conversations in our personal or professional lives, or suddenly ghosting someone we're in conflict with rather than meeting up to address the problem. Even if our usual go-to survival instinct is to fight, we may shift into flight mode whenever we're confronted with a threat that feels too big to tackle head-on.

When my previous husband and I were going through our divorce, we lived in the very small town in Northern California where he had been born and raised and where his family and wide circle of his friends still lived. Living alone for the first time in years, I immersed myself in spiritual studies with the clear intention of bringing a new, more self-loving and expansive vibration into my life. But every time I went into town, I would encounter what felt like a very real threat to the spiritual progress I was trying so hard to make. Everywhere I went—be it to the grocery store, the bookstore, or the gym—I ran into one of his family members or friends, who seemed to pop up around every corner, and found myself hurrying through errands in an attempt to avoid them. As you might expect, all of them had taken my ex's side in the divorce and held me in a not-so-favorable light; some of them even openly criticized or ridiculed me. It was hurtful and very uncomfortable.

I couldn't very well ask all of them to pack up and leave town, and I had no interest in either trying to change their opinion of me or in becoming a recluse. And so, my flight instinct kicked in and urged me to take a job in Philadelphia, Pennsylvania—nearly as far away from that small California town as one can possibly get without leaving the United States. In this instance, my flight instinct happened to align with my soul's calling: That single, cross-country move ushered in a whole series of events that not only massively catapulted my spiritual growth but ultimately led me to meet my now-husband and soulmate. But it doesn't always work this way. In fact, sometimes our flight survival response causes us to avoid, suppress, or deny our next evolution that is wanting to come forth.

Our flight instinct may keep us running from mounting evidence that something in our lives needs to change, rather than following the flow of our own inspiration and intuition. An impulse arises within us, clear as a bell, to do or not do something, to take a certain action or pursue a particular path, but instead of moving with it in flow, we resist the impulse out of fear. We might even deny ever having felt the impulse to move in a new direction because to follow it feels like a threat to the life we believe we're in control of. Or we may tell ourselves that it's just not that important or justify that it can wait until a more convenient time. Vices such as excessive use of stimulants, workaholism, or compulsive shopping, cleaning, gossiping, or busyness can also be manifestations of our body's survival instinct to flee. When we're in flight mode, we do anything and everything in our power to run away from or distract ourselves from the present moment.

When it comes to outrunning a hungry tiger, our flight response is invaluable, but it becomes a hindrance when it's triggered in situations that aren't actually life-threatening. The flight survival response is rooted in fear and a lack of trust in the universe. For example, if we were hurt by love in the past, we may run from intimacy in the present, fearing that we'll be hurt again. If money is not flowing as abundantly as we want or need, we might put off opening the bills that come in the mail rather than dealing with our creditors directly. In truth, an infinite number of new possibilities could unfold in every situation we walk into, with every person we interact with, and even within our own bodies and minds. But when out of fear we drag the past into the present, we flee from rather than open ourselves to these expanded possibilities. And sometimes, when we're suddenly or unexpectedly confronted by a potential threat, our brains may not have time or energy to launch a fight-or-flight response, and we collapse into freeze mode instead.

The Freeze Response

The high desert of Arizona where I live is filled with wild bunnies—as well as coyotes who would like nothing more than to make a meal out of them. Sometimes when a bunny is being chased by a coyote and senses it can't outrun the threat, it opts for a freeze survival response. It becomes like a statue and remains perfectly still, its features seamlessly blending into the surrounding desert scape. But where bunnies and other animals have built-in camouflage that might make the freeze instinct successful, human beings do not.

All we're doing is delaying the inevitable. Unlike bunnies hiding for their lives, our physical survival is not often what is in question when the freeze response hits us. Sometimes we freeze because we're caught off guard by something that challenges our physical or emotional security and we're instinctively trying to buy ourselves some time to figure out how best to respond. We check out, mentally and emotionally, effectively putting our bodies and minds into a sort of shutdown mode, so we can avoid feeling the inevitable pain of the present moment.

I remember sitting around the dinner table with my family one Christmas Eve when my mom made a particularly critical and rude remark that caught everyone off guard. Unsure of what else to do, my dad, uncle, and I all froze, forks in mid-transit to our mouths, unconsciously trying to make ourselves invisible and hoping the discomfort of that moment would somehow go away. Our physical survival was never in question, but my mother's volatility communicated to my family members and me that our emotional safety was very much on the line. This is our body's freeze instinct on full display.

When launched in response to a threatening or troubling situation, our freeze survival instinct causes us to become paralyzed, disoriented, disengaged, or numb, both mentally and physically, and rather than fight or flee, we're compelled to stay put or keep quiet, hoping that the stressful situation will simply pass us by. In everyday situations, this can manifest as avoiding the very actions we know will move us in the direction of what we want: communicating our feelings, setting an important boundary, initiating a conversation about a pay raise at work, or asking for more of what we desire in an intimate relationship.

When our freeze survival response is engaged, we may turn to vices such as overeating, oversleeping, watching excessive TV, or taking drugs or alcohol to numb our feelings of discomfort rather than using our pain as information to help us decipher where we have stumbled out of frequency with our souls. The freeze response shuts us down and causes us to lose touch with the subtle fluctuations of what's happening in our inner world. It prevents us from hearing the voice of our own intuition and makes flow state—in that moment, at least—unreachable.

Sometimes we perceive our adversary as having so much power that fighting, fleeing, or freezing do not seem like viable options to keep us safe. In this case, we may turn in desperation to a fawn response.

The Fawn Response

The fawn response—a term coined by psychologist Pete Walker—describes our compulsion to charm, please, appease, or pacify someone we perceive as a threat as a strategy to keep them from hurting us. This instinct compels us to become overly nice or accommodating—even at the cost of our own needs, preferences, or desires. As Walker explained in his 2013 book, *Complex PTSD*, "Fawn types seek safety by merging with the wishes, needs, and demands of others. They act as if they unconsciously believe that the price of admission to any relationship is the forfeiture of all their needs, rights, preferences, and boundaries." Excessive apologizing, habitual people-pleasing, nervous chitchat, and self-deprecation, as well as difficulty upholding personal boundaries and being unable or unwilling to express our own needs, are all signs that our fawn survival mechanism is currently engaged and running the show.

Fawn is a state of hypervigilance in which we place other people's needs above our own, leaving us feeling ungrounded, undernourished, and unsteady. Rather than prioritizing our own connection with Source energy, we prioritize other people's feelings, the "shoulds" of life, duties, or outworn commitments that no longer serve us. Even worse than us not prioritizing feeling good, we can actually become accustomed to feeling bad. On this point, I vividly recall a scene described by a participant in one of my healing retreats years ago, which perfectly captures the way we block ourselves from the abundant flow of life force energy when we slip into fawn mode.

This beautiful young woman—I'll call her Anna—was a stay-at-home mom to three children. While sharing with our circle of women, she described the tension that she experienced each night when her husband, Marc, returned home from work. She told us that he was almost always critical and demanding and that she would spend a good part of her days thinking of ways to please him and hopefully lift his spirits when the family spent time together in the evenings. Some of her go-to strategies were to put on music, offer him a martini the moment he walked through the door, and make one of his favorite meals for dinner. Yet each night after dinner, and despite all her efforts, Marc's sour mood persisted, and he would invariably retreat to his man cave in the garage, where he would play guitar and smoke cigars until well after she'd cleared the dinner table and put the children to bed.

Anna was convinced that her survival (and the survival of her children) depended on Marc, and this perception kept her replaying the same subservient role, which left her feeling powerless and angry every night when she went to bed. Over the course of our work together, as she began to soothe her nervous system and develop awareness about the triggers that caused her to launch into fawn mode, she discovered more direct ways of communicating her desires that actually got Marc's attention and allowed herself to finally admit that she desired a more respectful and attentive life partner.

As Anna's story illustrates, when we're in fawn mode, we can easily lose sight of our needs in favor of tending to the needs of another, and this makes us susceptible to codependent or toxic relationships in both our personal and professional lives. Our fawn

Faces of Resistance: Fight, Flight, Freeze, and Fawn

instinct tells us over and over not to rock the boat, that it's safer to make ourselves feel uncomfortable than to risk making the other person uncomfortable, particularly those upon whom we feel our survival (physical, emotional, social, or financial) depends.

These fight, flight, freeze, or fawn instincts might be nature's way of ensuring our survival, but they are strategies that were intended to be short-lived—to give us the temporary burst of adrenaline needed to outrun a hungry predator or the chance to hide from an angry adversary, for example. Now that life and our daily circumstances have changed and grown more complex, the sad reality is that the majority of us are trapped in a vibration of fight, flight, freeze, or fawn. We're living in a chronic state of fear and reactivity, outside the stream of flow.

For the duration of time that any of our survival instincts are informing our consciousness, we lose sight of the fact that we are literally Spirit incarnated in human form, an inseparable part of a universe too infinite and intelligent to even comprehend, born with the power to receive, contain, and transmit the energy that orchestrates all things at our fingertips. In survival mode, we don't feel like powerful creators; we feel more like primitive animals, constantly affected by the world around us, and our only choice is to prepare for battle or to passively submit. Temporarily displaced from our innate power to create our own reality, we believe that our only path to regaining any control over our lives is by getting someone or something else to change. *If this person would just be different, then I would be in flow*, we think. *If he would just stop being moody . . . If she would just become more responsible . . . If my boss would just acknowledge my value . . . If my spouse would just make more money . . . If they would just change, then I could be happy; then I would be at peace; then I would be in flow.*

A lifetime spent in survival mode trains us to believe that our only shot at success, happiness, love, or any of the other experiences we desire is to control the people and circumstances around us—or to control the contrast that is an inevitable part of life. Of course, it doesn't take very much life experience for us to discover that we can't control the people, events, and contrast that surround us. That doesn't keep us from trying, now, does it? And this only amplifies our feelings of frustration and vulnerability.

Surviving but Not Thriving

This is why—mentally, emotionally, and physically—most of us go through our days feeling gnarled up with tension, tightly wound, and hyper-alert, just waiting for the proverbial other shoe to drop. Yes, we're surviving, but we're certainly not thriving, and we greet the painful and even the pleasurable moments with struggle, distrust, fear, and resistance, rather than a felt sense that we are flowing along a joyful, abundant, and effortless current of well-being.

When the limbic system is in control, it's like we go into a mental spiral where the only options we can see are those that will help us to get through the immediacy of an unpleasant situation. We can't see what is in the highest or best interest of ourselves or the other person. We can't hear what our hearts really want, and we can't make out what a mutually beneficial solution would even look like. All that our consciousness can conceive of in those moments is acting out some variation of these four primitive responses: fight, flight, freeze, or fawn.

So, how does this detailed description of our primitive survival mechanisms square with the idea that we are all born with free will?

In the previous chapter, we explored that the reason we have access to free will at every level of our consciousness is because there is always a space between stimulus—what happens to us—and our response to that stimulus. In that space between stimulus and response lies our power to choose our perspective, our thoughts, our feelings, our words, and our actions. In other words, in that space lies our power to create our own reality, independent of the circumstances that surround us. I shared examples from my own life and from the lives of some extraordinary human beings like Viktor Frankl and Mahatma Gandhi, who found a way to tap into that space and exercise the power of their own free will, even when the circumstances that surrounded them were painfully oppressive.

So, if there is a space between stimulus and response (and there is!), then why don't we hang out in that space 24/7, so we can choose our responses on purpose and deliberately create the reality we desire? The answer is that we shrink that space and limit our access to our own free will on a daily basis. How exactly we do this is a fascinating process that we'll get to in a moment.

In fact, when our nervous system is in fight, flight, freeze, or fawn mode, our perception of the space between stimulus and response shrinks so drastically that we sometimes forget it's even there at all. In survival mode, the freight train of our perception giving rise to thoughts, which then trigger emotions, which then motivate us to speak and act in certain predictable ways, comes barreling down the track of our nervous system at lightning speed. Someone we care about says or does something we don't like, and within a millisecond, we're insulted, hurt, defeated, or enraged. Suddenly we're unconsciously marshaling our forces to escape, appease, or do battle with that person as though our very survival was at stake. Why?

Neurons That Fire Together Wire Together

The human brain is an unbelievably efficient machine. Whatever it can automate, it will. With every action you take, your brain evaluates: *Is this something I am likely to repeat again?* If the answer is yes, it outsources the work of that action to the subconscious mind, making it essentially automatic. Your brain's ability to automate your repetitive actions explains how you can sometimes find yourself miles down the road on your way to work without any awareness of having driven there. Your subconscious already knows how to get you to your destination, leaving your conscious mind free to contemplate more pressing issues. The same thing happens with other habitual actions like closing the garage door when you arrive home from work or brushing your teeth every night with your dominant hand. Sometimes these actions are so unconscious—so automatic—that you find yourself questioning if you actually did them. This is exactly what happens with our automatic emotional reactions.

Every time we lock onto a perception, have a thought, experience an emotion, or take an action that is automatic and instinctive, we are wiring our neural circuitry to perform this reaction even more efficiently and with less conscious awareness on our part. This is because the more routine a pattern of thought or behavior becomes, the less aware we are of it. *Did I turn off the stove before I left the house? Did I lock the door?* This loss of surveillance not only can interfere with our daily functioning, but can allow bad habits to creep up on us. Think of a person who complains about feeling stiff or out of shape. At first, the choice to relax on the couch rather than go out for a walk is so subtle that it goes unnoticed. It's only when that person finds themselves unable to touch their toes or breathless after climbing a few flights of stairs that they recognize the cumulative effect of that single daily choice. The concept that habitual behaviors create pathways in our brains that grow deeper and wider every time we repeat them was introduced by Canadian neuropsychologist Donald Hebb in his 1949 book, *The Organization of Behavior: A Neuropsychological Theory*. Hebb's theory, that repeated activation of neurons strengthens the connections between them, laid the foundation for the cutting-edge science of neuroplasticity and later became simplified into the phrase "neurons that fire together wire together."

When you engage the same reaction to something every day or three times a week—such as fawning each time you get on the phone with a parent because you don't have the energy to put up a boundary—your brain eventually learns to automate that process to save you the mental energy of having to decide how to behave all over again. Over time, your brain gets so good at triggering that reaction that you don't even realize you're doing it. And the more frequently you react that way, the more attractive that neural pathway becomes—and the more likely you are to use it. A self-fulfilling prophesy, anyone?

In permitting our nervous system to travel down the same well-trodden reactive pathways, we are essentially shrinking the space between stimulus and response and limiting our own access to free will. We are Spirit-infused human beings, capable in every moment of weighing our options, seeking out new perspectives, educating ourselves on other ways of responding, and innovating brand-new solutions to even our most long-standing problems, aka creating new and healthier neural pathways in our brains to travel on. When we're guided only by our automatic and unconscious wiring, we limit ourselves to the same primitive range of choices available to animals.

Watch a documentary about gorillas or chimpanzees, and you'll notice right away how many similarities there are between us and them: their hands, feet, and faces; their feeding and grooming habits; the way they laugh and smile; and the compassion in their eyes are all so incredibly human. But the fact is that we are separated from these primates and their ancestors by literally millions of years of evolution—most of which occurred in the realm of our cognition.

Whereas those primates are wired to act without hesitation on every survival impulse, human beings have the unique ability to contemplate the repercussions of an action before we jump into it. We humans are designed with the gift of self-awareness, which means we understand—intellectually, at least—that our immediate perspective is not the only one available, and in fact, there are as many different ways to perceive something as there are people living in the world.

Unlike other animals, we have the capacity to evaluate a course of action, not just in terms of its ability to guarantee us another night of safety within our community but also in terms of its ability to yield long-term happiness, freedom, and prosperity. And unlike other primates, human beings are capable of abstract thinking and vision-oriented planning. We can use our free will to delay immediate gratification and choose instead to work toward a future reward. In other words, we can consciously decide to pause in the space between stimulus and response, and the more often we do this, the wider that space becomes and the more choices become available to us in each moment.

Faces of Resistance: Fight, Flight, Freeze, and Fawn

Widening the Gap Between Stimulus and Response

So, what does it look like—in a practical sense—to widen the space between stimulus and response? To get a sense of this, first identify a common trigger that normally sends you into fight, flight, freeze, or fawn mode. This could be a blunt coworker, a text message that you perceive as being rude or dismissive, or even a notification on your phone that usually brings up a feeling of worry or dread. Then, instead of immediately engaging with that stimulus—in this analogy, attending to the notification on your phone—do three things to restore some balance in your nervous system. First, take one deep, full breath, with an audible exhale, if you can. Next, sit back in your chair, or rest a little further back on your heels, and feel your shoulders falling away from your ears. Last, feel your heart fill as you take a moment to acknowledge both your strength as well as all the things in your life that are going exceedingly, supremely well. Now, attend to whatever needs your attention.

Moments like these may seem insignificant, and in and of themselves, maybe they are. But moments like these, where we consciously linger a little longer in that potent space between stimulus and response, stack into hours that build into days. And it's in these momentary increments that we begin to reassume control of our own nervous system and get back into the deliberate creator-driver's seat of our lives.

We widen the gap between stimulus and response by giving ourselves time to pause before committing to a particular course of action. So, before immediately firing back the next time you're confronted by a situation that feels threating to your physical, social, emotional, or financial security—say, for example, receiving a higher-than-expected bill from a trusted handyman—pause long enough to notice the huge range of choices that you could, in fact, decide to make or not make in response. Yes, you could fight by aggressively lashing out and attempting to invalidate or discredit the person or their work. Yes, you could flee by ripping the bill up or shoving it into a drawer so you no longer see it. Yes, you could freeze by attempting to numb your discomfort with any number of vices and passively hope the problem will just go away. Yes, you could fawn by attempting to woo this person into giving you a discount, perhaps with the promise of sending referrals his or her way. Or you could remain focused on the only thing you ever have any control over—your own state of consciousness. You could choose, in that very moment of discomfort, to stay in the vibration of flow by focusing on what you *want* rather than on what currently is. You could bask in the fact that you alone have the power to decide how you will perceive and interpret this situation, and that you are the only one who can determine the direction of your own thoughts, feelings, words, and actions. You could decide not to waste one precious ounce of your energy attempting to control what is outside your control, and that certainly includes this hypothetical situation. You could choose not to become swept up in what this or any other person is doing or creating. You could remind yourself that everyone is creating from their own state of consciousness, which has nothing to do with yours, and that other people cannot create inside of your reality, just as you cannot create inside of theirs. You could notice the moment when your animal instincts begin to sway your perceptions, thoughts, feelings, words, or actions down the path toward an undesired destination and make the conscious choice to back away from that ledge.

We have all found ourselves in situations in which we feel backed into a corner, where circumstances loom so large that we feel we have no other choice but to react. In moments like these, it can be so tempting to hit the metaphoric Screw This button and haul off on

Faces of Resistance: Fight, Flight, Freeze, and Fawn

one of numerous automatic thoughts, moods, words, or behaviors in order to discharge our stress. But even in high-pressure situations like these, self-awareness reminds us that we have access to an entire circuit board of choices that we could make instead. We could just as easily choose the Breathe Deeply button, the Go for a Walk button, the Soak in a Hot Bath button, or the Call a Friend button. These higher choices come into view only when we've given ourselves a moment to pause in the space between stimulus and response. Only then are we calm enough to register them.

Now that we've laid the foundation for understanding our primitive survival reactions in a general sense, it's time to explore which of these roles has been the most deeply hardwired into your nervous system. All of us have been touched by life in unique ways. We were all born with certain talents and shortcomings, we each inherited certain advantages and disadvantages, and we've all endured our share of trauma—both the Big-T and little-t varieties. All of these experiences have colored the lenses through which we perceive life and have conditioned our nervous system to react in certain reflexive ways. Understanding our unique energetic imprints and emotional triggers is essential to freeing ourselves to make more powerful choices.

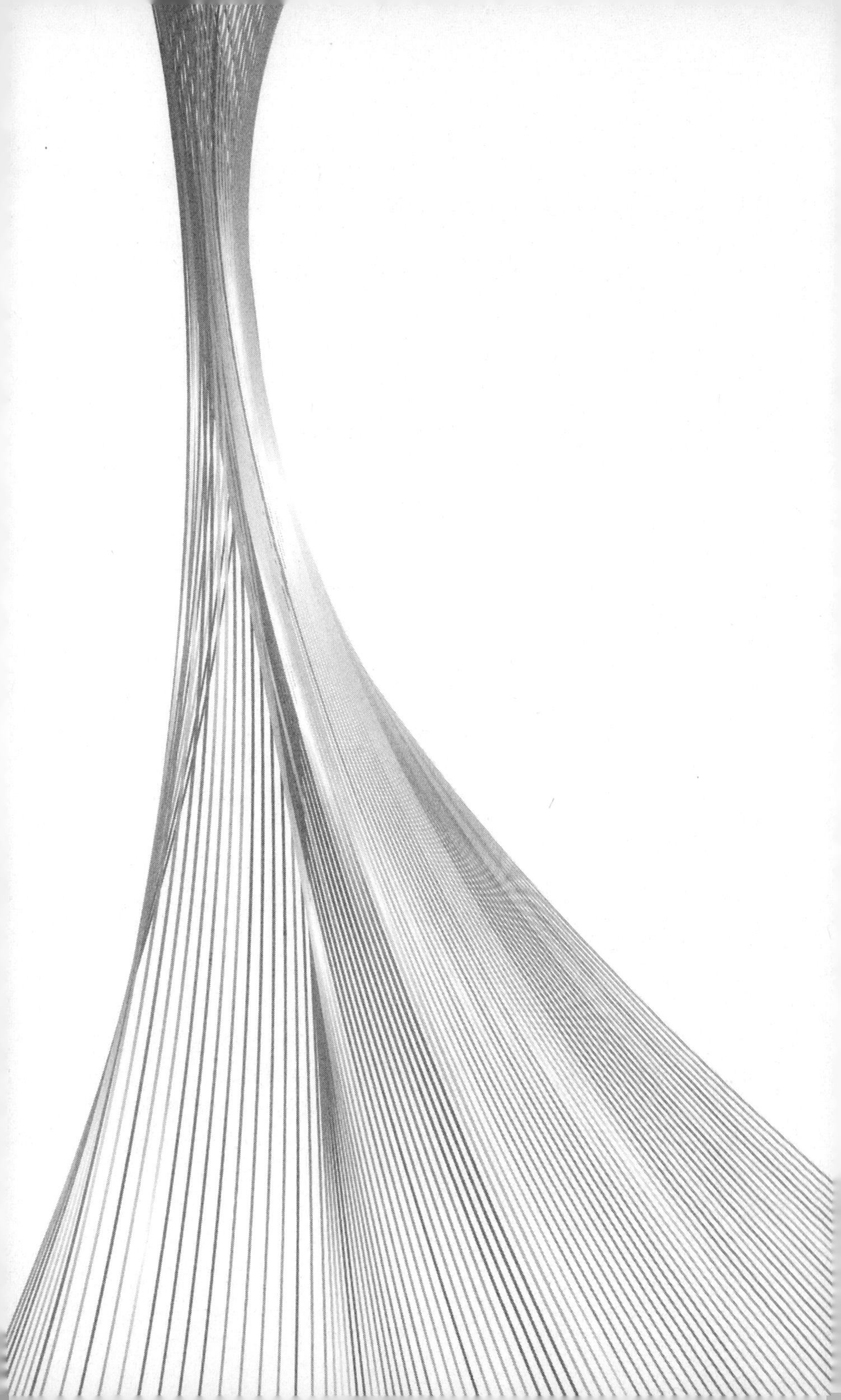

4

Energetic Imprints and Emotional Triggers

Before we go further, let's back up just a bit so that you can consider the conversation we're about to have on the topic of energetic imprints and emotional triggers within a broader context.

At the basis of everything about you that feels fixed or static is a constantly flowing and changing stream of energy—and the same stream of energy that flows through you flows through every living thing in this universe. The energy current that causes your heart to beat, your lungs to breathe, and your muscles to move also encourages plants to grow toward the sun and orchestrates the planets of our solar system to orbit in harmony with each another around that sun. There is only one stream of energy, and it's a divine stream, a stream of abundance, a stream of well-being—a stream of flow. This stream of energy flows in only one direction, which is toward the infinite expansion of all that you are.

Wow. Take a moment to read that paragraph again because this is the intersection where spirituality, science, and quantum physics all come together and reveal that literally *everything* is energy.

When you are in harmony with this stream, you are in a state of flow, and you experience everything you consider to be good or joyful or satisfying or wanted. When you're out of harmony with this stream of universal energy, you experience feeling blocked, stuck, frustrated, fearful, powerless—everything you consider to be unwanted, unpleasant, or bad. Here's the thing to always keep in mind: You are this energy stream, and you're also the one who is experiencing this energy as either flowing or stuck!

You are divine energy, temporarily inhabiting the suit of flesh and bone that you call your physical body—a physical body that came hardwired with certain instincts to help keep you alive. For example, you have sensors built into your skin that alert you when something you're about to touch is too hot, too cold, or just right. You have instincts built into your nervous system that circulate through your body by way of neurochemicals like adrenaline and dopamine and that alert you to potential rewards and dangers alike. And because your brain is one of the most highly intelligent and constantly learning machines in all of the universe, it's been keeping a keen record of everything you have ever experienced, noting which events brought you joy and satisfaction, which were neutral and therefore unremarkable, and which brought you pain or deprivation. As a result of your very specific collection of life experiences, your brain and nervous system have constructed a very specific plan for keeping you safe, sound, healthy, and whole. So far, so good, right?

Right! Our human instincts are extremely beneficial because their very purpose is to keep us alive. But for far too many of us, these instincts have gone from serving as a backup, emergency support system to becoming the primary map we use to navigate our life. We have all but forgotten about the stream of well-being that is always available to guide us along a path of flow. We have forgotten that we are cosmic beings here to surf all the delicious waves of experiences this world has to offer. We have forgotten that we hold within us the power to master our own energy and therefore to perceive any condition as a blessing rather than as a curse, and to remain neutral rather than take life personally. We have forgotten that we are here to make our desires manifest—to live in a stream of affluence in all our worldly endeavors, simply because we are connected to and a part of the energetic flow of All That Is. In other words, we have come to think of ourselves as this temporary suit of flesh, bones, and nerves rather than as the infinite stream of energy that we really are. Instead of surfing the waves of life, using even the turbulent ones to catapult us toward more of what we desire, we come to live in fear of them. We forget that we are divine beings who have incarnated into this three-dimensional world to take delight in every facet of human experience, even the contrasting ones. Most of us have forgotten that thriving in a state of flow is our divine birthright, and so we resign ourselves to spending—ahem, *wasting*—our life just struggling to survive. To say this in the simplest terms possible, instead of flowing our attention toward what we do want, most of us have become conditioned to run from, push away, or otherwise resist the things we do not want.

So, anytime we encounter conflict, we lean into our survival instincts. We fight, which is to say we attempt to control the flow of life through aggression, demands, wielding power, or throwing fits. We flee, meaning we attempt to find flow by avoiding whatever or whomever seems to be opposing us at any given moment. We freeze, meaning we temporarily take ourselves out of the game of life by pulling the covers over our heads, so to speak, and numbing ourselves in any of a dozen different ways. Or we fawn, meaning we try to charm, cajole, and manipulate the flow of life to our liking by appearing to be interested, helpful, accommodating, or charismatic.

In the previous chapter, we talked in-depth about each of these four primary faces of resistance, which our instincts urge us to launch into anytime we feel our physical, emotional, social, or financial survival is being threatened. In this chapter, we're going to examine why each of us is wired toward one of these primitive reactions over another. When faced with conflict or opposition to something we desire, why do some of us aggressively gear up for battle while others freeze in fear? Why are some of us more prone to people-pleasing, while others look for safety by withdrawing from people altogether? To answer these questions, we need to understand the energetic dynamics that played out in our formative years—within our families of origin and extended families, with our peer groups and teachers and mentors, and within the broader communities that we identified as being "our people."

The "Garden" of Your Early Life

For this discussion, I'd like you to think of the early influences in your life as the unique ecosystem that you were born and raised in. Like a garden, your childhood had its own climate, its own seasons, and its own storm systems. It was an environment that grew both flowers and weeds.

Like plants need water, sunlight, and fertile soil to grow, all children need to know that we are unconditionally accepted and loved by our caregivers, without having to earn that love and acceptance. We need to know that nothing we could ever say, do, or not do will cause us to lose the love of our caregivers. We need to be allowed to feel and communicate the full range of our human emotions

Energetic Imprints and Emotional Triggers

without shame, to express our individuality, and to engage in free, spontaneous play. If we don't get these basic needs met as children, we mature with a diminished sense of self that is not secure or stable but easily shaken and therefore underdeveloped and undernourished, like a piece of fruit that withers on the vine due to lack of water.

You can think of the soil you were raised in as a young plant, so to speak, as being abundant in some of these vital minerals but deficient in others. In your case, it could be that you were given every nutrient you could possibly need to thrive, to the point that you felt suffocated and rejected it all to protect your own autonomy. Or maybe the ground you were planted in was so dry and depleted that it could barely support life. Maybe the garden of your most formative years was surrounded or even invaded by malicious weeds or poisoned by other toxins that leached into the soil. It's vital to understand that in the same way a plant absorbs water and light, as children, we take on and absorb—literally metabolize into ourselves—the vibrations of those around us. We didn't just absorb the energy of love and caring that was transmitted to us by our parents, families, teachers, siblings, and friends—we also absorbed the energy of their unprocessed emotions, their unhealed wounds and attachment disorders, their addictions, their fears, and their frustrated desires. These vibrations became mixed into the very soil that fed us. And to all these vibrations—the good, the bad, and the ugly—we had to figure out how to adapt in order to survive.

For example, I adapted to the environment in my family of origin by identifying as a rebel and a fighter. I knew from a very early age that I did not want to follow in the footsteps of my parents, who tended to view themselves as victims of life's challenges. I also knew that I did not want to follow in the footsteps of my older sister, who either froze up or tried to run from problems rather than confront them head-on. In response to these and other early life experiences, I became someone who speaks up for what I wanted. I would call out pettiness and small thinking when I saw it. I would assertively go after the things I wanted rather than passively waiting or hoping for them to happen and then feel like a victim of life when they did not simply fall into my lap. Identifying myself as a fighter rather than a victim had both its benefits and its challenges, as does every role we assume early on to help us survive. In this chapter, I'm going to ask you to explore the forces and vibrations from your childhood that shaped your early identity because—unless you have healed or processed them to the point that you now hold them in absolute compassion and appreciation—it's very likely that these vibrations are still active in your life today.

What roles did you witness being played out among the cast of characters in your early life? Did Mom stand her ground when life became stressful, or did she take off, either physically or emotionally? Was Dad usually the aggressor or the victim? And what about you? Did you most frequently play the part of the golden child, the problem child, or the lost child? Or were you cast in the role of Mother's Little Helper, whose job was to be the glue that held everyone together or who needed to put on a cheerful face to keep the peace? In response to the dynamics you witnessed early on, did you learn to fight back by becoming rebellious? Did you feel it was your job to fix things that were broken, or did you perpetually feel betrayed and mistreated by other people's behaviors? Or maybe a combination of all of them?

This was the vibrational garden that you were raised in, and no matter how many hours you have logged in meditation or how much therapy you have done, these early impressions still exist within you, shaping your current perceptions, thoughts, feelings, words and actions. Once you have a clear idea of the energetic dynamics that influenced your consciousness early on in your life, you can then decide whether your adaptations to those dynamics are still serving you today. Helping you reach that understanding is the purpose of this chapter.

A Vibrational Understanding of Trauma

As we've discussed previously in this book, and in all my other books, we are energetic receivers, containers, and transmitters, which means we are constantly exchanging information and energy with everything and everyone around us. Nowhere in our life is this more apparent than in our relationships with other people. As sensitive energetic receivers, we do more than simply observe the look, the scent, the body language, and the presence of a person who has just entered our space. We soak them in on an energetic, vibrational level.

At a level far more powerful than words, or anything that can be registered with any of our five senses, we are receiving the energetic wavelengths of each person, and those wavelengths are mingling with and entraining with our own. Most of us intuitively understand this. When as adults we encounter a person who is really angry or if someone in our presence is in a lot of pain, we get it and we feel it, but we don't necessarily take it personally or take their energy on. We simply observe it as a stream of energy that has entered our space, and we have some measure of personal agency as to how we respond to that energy.

As children, we didn't perceive a hard boundary between ourselves and our parents, grandparents, teachers, or siblings. Their energy was simply the sea we were swimming in; the garden we were growing in. The vibrations of our parents, our home, our classrooms, and our communities mingled with our own, and we took everything very, very personally. Remember that as young children, we are powerless—not in a metaphoric sense but in a very literal one. Because our lives are in fact at stake in our early years, our powerful survival instincts kick in, demanding that we adapt to and play along with those around us, no matter how messed up they were. This is where the distinction between Big-T and little-t trauma, which I touched on earlier in this book, comes in.

Just for point of reference, the DSM-5, which is considered the authoritative guide to diagnosing mental disorders, defines trauma as "any situation where one's life or bodily integrity is threatened" (American Psychiatric Association, 2013). However, thanks to the pioneering work of people like Francine Shapiro, the psychologist and educator who created a trauma treatment called Eye Movement Desensitization and Reprocessing (EMDR), we now understand that trauma comes in all shapes and sizes and is certainly not limited to physical threats alone. This definition of trauma is often more related to the Big-T traumas, such as experiencing combat or war, assault, natural disasters, and more. Little-t traumas that are born out of chronic stress, emotional abandonment, or neglect can cause significant psychological distress and therefore make a serious impact on our developing sense of self. In her 2012 book, *Getting Past Your Past*, Shapiro explained that "everyday life experiences,

Energetic Imprints and Emotional Triggers

such as relationship problems or unemployment, can produce just as many, and sometimes even more, symptoms of PTSD."

Little-t traumas include things like being bullied; dealing with racism, exclusion, or cliques at school; witnessing addiction, animosity, infidelity, or divorce within your home; experiencing the sudden loss of a family member or beloved pet; living with the knowledge that your parents were under severe financial pressures or facing legal troubles; or being separated from your family suddenly, without explanation, or for an extended period of time.

On a side note, as children, we almost always dismiss or deeply bury the feelings associated with both Big-T and little-t traumas alike—either because our survival demanded that we minimize them or because we were simply not yet developmentally capable of processing those feelings at the time. But the energy of these impactful experiences stays with us, locked into both our unconscious minds and our muscle memory, and will continually seek out ways to be released. We'll explore this concept more in the next chapter.

Of course, as adults, we understand that all these little-t traumatic events are simply part of life: People get divorced, peers can be cruel, loved ones die, and families relocate or must sometimes live apart. Once we're parents ourselves, we understand all too well that sometimes life's demands are such that we just can't pick up our child every time they cry, and sometimes we feel we have no other choice but to leave our children for a time in a less-than-ideal environment. As adults, we understand this, but as children who are utterly dependent on our caregivers to feed, shelter, clothe, love, and accept us, we take everything personally.

Even if our childhoods were relatively "normal," we still grew up in the vibrational atmosphere of human beings who, even on their best days, probably had no idea how to manage their thoughts or master their own energy. Unless you were a very rare exception, your parents likely knew no other option but to allow their emotions to run wild or to numb or bury them altogether. Like most people, they probably felt powerless over life's circumstances and tried to run from—rather than feel, understand, and release—their suffering. When our parents were faced with adversity, most of us watched them spiral into drama, blaming, feeling victimized by, or caretaking other people at the expense of their own well-being, not because they were bad people, but simply because they knew no other way. We watched them turn to vices or become workaholics, perhaps until they reached their own mental or physical breaking point. In many cases, they blamed us, not because they genuinely believed we were at fault but because their own energy bodies were so blocked up and their nervous systems so dysregulated that we became a convenient dumping ground to offload some of their stress. The point is, very few of us were raised by parents who prioritized their own emotional and energetic regulation. As a result, very few of us are adults who embody true emotional intelligence, who know how to properly master and regulate our emotions.

Within our families of origin—and later, within our classrooms, sports teams, peer groups, intimate relationships, workplace, and so on—it's as if we find ourselves starring in a drama alongside a cast of characters handpicked to shine a spotlight on both our strengths and our weaknesses. Just think back to your earliest recollection of your own childhood dynamics and notice the different roles that the significant people in your life have played. Was there a narcissist, someone who made it all about themselves and whom you felt you had to tiptoe around or try to pacify or please? Was there a scapegoat, who continually got into trouble or brought your mood down? Was there someone who suffered from addiction or who seemed always to be sick, suffering, or otherwise in a bad way, who frequently needed to be bailed out physically, financially, or energetically by the other people in the family? Was there an overachiever, a golden boy or girl who seemed to take the lion's share of the family's limelight, energy, support, or praise? And most importantly, within the interpersonal drama of your early years, what role did you learn to play to survive, physically, socially, and emotionally?

As you read this, just take a deep breath and begin to sense for yourself the roles and adaptations that were imprinted into your young nervous system in response to the behaviors and—more importantly—the vibrations being offered by those around you. Most likely, these adaptations fall into one of three very distinct roles.

The Drama Triangle, aka, the Triangle of Lack

In the late 1960s, psychiatrist Stephen Karpman published an article entitled "Fairy Tales and Script Drama Analysis" in the *Transactional Analysis Bulletin*, which introduced a revolutionary new model he hoped would shed some light on the dysfunctional roles that human beings tend to fall into during times of conflict. In this article, Karpman outlined three roles—that of the *Victim*, the *Persecutor*, and the *Rescuer*—which people often vacillate between in their interactions with one another. Years later, in 2014, Karpman wrote the book *A Game Free Life*, which provided a deeper exploration of these roles and their impact on relationships.

Karpman labeled this social model the "Drama Triangle," because anytime we find ourselves identified with one of these polarizing roles, we inevitably create a lot of unnecessary and painful drama. In my coaching and healing work with clients, I have come to refer to this model as the "Triangle of Lack" because I have discovered that the only times we fall into these limiting roles is when we're perceiving ourselves as lacking and powerless—that is, when we feel that our happiness, lovability, acceptance, or survival is dependent on another person, place, or thing. By whatever name you call it, the Drama Triangle or Triangle of Lack is a predictable, repetitive pattern anytime we're seeking power or validation from others. It's a misguided way of trying to manage our own resistance to life by controlling the people and circumstances around us. From an energy perspective, when we're caught in this triangle, we feel stuck and without options, and so we habitually act out one of these three disempowering roles in an attempt to relate to those around us.

There are three distinct roles or positions within the Triangle of Lack, and each of these enables and perpetuates the other two. As you read each of these descriptions from Karpman's Drama Triangle theory, notice if any (or all) of them take you back to the dynamics you witnessed between the key characters in your early childhood.

THE VICTIM

While all three roles within the Triangle of Lack experience themselves as powerless, the Victim feels especially so. Those identifying with the Victim role will see themselves as being at the mercy of whatever troubling circumstance they find themselves in. "Why me?" is the battle cry of those mired in the role of the Victim, who often alternate between rage and self-pity because they perceive themselves as powerless to effect change in their own lives.

They feel that things are happening *to* them not *for* them—as if the universe and everyone in it is out to get them. When confronted with potential danger or conflict, the Victim's tendency is to flee or freeze. They blame other people or life in general for their poor lot but rarely ask for help directly, preferring for others to guess what they need so they can be rescued from an unfair person or situation—or from themselves. They feel powerless to ask for help.

The "payoff" we seek in playing the Victim role is that we get to avoid taking responsibility for our own experience and instead cast other people, situations, or life in general in the role of the bad guy or the savior. The other payoff is that we get to make ourselves the center of other people's attention by portraying ourselves as wounded, oppressed, helpless, powerless, or weak.

THE PERSECUTOR

In every drama where there is a Victim who has been wronged by life, there must also be someone who is cast in the role of the "bad guy" or villain. Within the Triangle of Lack, the role of the villain is played by the Persecutor.

Those in the Persecutor role adopt a "fight" stance to gain control over a perceived conflict or threat. Persecutors posture themselves as the superior one in the situation and will criticize, adopt an authoritative stance, or make threats in order to defend their point of view or get their way. Feeling a sense of control and power is the primary payoff we seek in adopting the Persecutor role. Because we see ourselves as right and others as wrong, we feel justified in discharging our pent-up emotions—especially our anger and rage—on those we believe are to blame. The mantra of the Persecutor goes something like this: "This is all your fault," or "Now look what you made me do." The Persecutor role is a maladaptive way of seeking flow through control and intimidation.

THE RESCUER

While Victims seek energy through proclaiming their powerlessness and Persecutors feel energized by proving they are superior to others, Karpman believes that those in the role of the Rescuer relish the idea of being seen as the hero: the good person who swoops in to save the day.

When conflict such as an argument arises in the presence of someone who's identified with being a Rescuer, they can hardly control the urge to jump in, fix, change, or alter the current situation, even if those involved in the drama have not asked for—or downright do not want—their help. In fact, Rescuers often feel an obligation to help even when they themselves don't want to, and they may find themselves doing things for other people that they haven't been asked to do—and then feel resentful or victimized if they are not appreciated for their efforts. This dynamic gives you some insight into how easily we can move from role to role once we're caught up in the Triangle of Lack. More on this in a moment.

Rescuers are often fawn types who seek a payoff by garnering energy from the external acceptance, love, and praise of those they help and save. As a result, they tend to continually attract those they sense need their wisdom or assistance. At the same time, Rescuers are deeply uncomfortable with conflict and throw themselves into the helper role to avoid that discomfort. While on the surface this may seem noble, the Rescuer enables all participants in the Triangle of Lack to remain locked in their roles. This brings up an important point: All the roles within the Triangle of Lack are interchangeable, in the sense that each one perpetuates the next. Say, in one interaction, one person plays the role of Rescuer, trying to help someone who's identified as a Victim. And then in the very next moment, the

Rescuer suddenly becomes the Victim, while the former Victim becomes the Persecutor. Let me give you an example.

Many years ago, I was at dinner with an old family friend who began complaining about how much weight she had gained and told us all that no matter what she did or how hard she tried, she simply couldn't lose it. My husband, whom everyone regarded as the "glue" in his family, jumped in to help her, offering the services of a friend of ours who works as a personal trainer. Now cast in his familiar Rescuer role, Frederic agreed to set everything up with our personal trainer friend and to pay for the first few sessions.

As I watched this scenario unfolding, I knew that Frederic's offer to help—while well-intentioned—would come back to bite him in the butt. I knew this because I understand that those caught in the role of Victim are not actually looking for help. They are looking for someone or something to blame for their situation, and Frederic had unwittingly fallen into this trap.

True to his word, Frederic made all the arrangements with our personal trainer and paid her in advance for creating a meal plan and a three-day-a-week exercise program for our friend. But when the time came for their first training session, our friend didn't show up. Now Frederic, who had just been in the role of Rescuer and had sincerely wanted to help, ended up feeling like the Victim because he put in time, money, and effort, only to find out that our friend had wasted all of it. When he confronted our friend about her missed appointment, she then donned the role of the Persecutor, saying, "Stop trying to fix me! I never asked for your help." This is how easily one role morphs into the next when we're caught in the Triangle of Lack. Everyone in it is in a state of lack, disconnected from the abundant energy of flow, so everyone in it ends up feeling powerless and bad.

Pay attention when people are acting out one of the roles in the Triangle of Lack and you will see that it's all about one person knowingly or unknowingly trying to siphon energy or power from another. We enact these dramas to attempt to heal some core wound—to feel loved, to feel secure, to feel important; to feel like we matter and have purpose. Victims feel temporarily soothed and therefore powerful when they succeed at being the center of attention, even if the only attention they're getting is pity. Persecutors feel powerful when they successfully dominate others into yielding to their opinion or their way. And Rescuers feel worthwhile and powerful when they've proved themselves useful and needed.

On the surface, the words and actions we use when we're in the Triangle of Lack can appear justified, valiant, even heroic. But I want you to be able to distinguish the fact that they are not. They are rooted in lack and powerlessness. When we sink into any of these three roles, it's as if we are saying, "I don't believe that I have what it takes to find my own flow and create my own abundance; therefore, I will look for power, approval, resources, and safety from you." As we've already discussed, this almost always goes back to unprocessed childhood wounds that have not been healed or to a significant time in our past when we were dependent on another person in some way and did have to adapt in order to survive. The Triangle of Lack is the dance that most human beings engage in—not just in relationship with each other but in relationship with life itself—with money, with success, with institutions, and even with our own bodies.

In the case of the family friend I just told you about, who is physically healthy in every way and yet chronically complains about not being able to lose weight, can you see how she resides inside the Triangle of Lack in relation to her own body? She's cast her body as the Persecutor—the one who is willfully not giving her what she wants—while she is the helpless Victim, powerless to do anything but complain. We all do this to some extent. We feel victimized by some condition that we feel powerless to change; then we either

Energetic Imprints and Emotional Triggers

persecute ourselves for not doing better or look for someone to rescue us or to listen to us vent about how the circumstances in which we find ourselves are not our fault.

We can also slip into the Triangle of Lack in relation to our careers, feeling victimized for having to work so hard or for not receiving the financial compensation or appreciation we feel we deserve. We then cast the various other players at work as the "bad guys" who don't appreciate or promote us. From this distorted viewpoint, we then look to someone or something outside of ourselves to rescue us and begin fantasizing that if only we worked for a different company or had a different boss, we would feel happier and more satisfied. This "if only . . . " way of thinking, by the way, is your first clue that you've entered the Triangle of Lack. Anytime we think someone or something outside of ourselves will finally rescue us and make us happy, satisfied, or fulfilled, we can be sure we are caught up in the Triangle of Lack.

I bring your awareness to these very common patterns that occur in our interactions with other people because whenever you find yourself slipping into one of these roles or see someone else acting them out, you can know one thing for sure—in this moment, the person who is acting out the Victim, the Perpetrator, or the Rescuer role is deeply triggered. They are feeling threatened and stuck. They are caught in a mindset of lack and are therefore perceiving life through the distorted lens that their physical, emotional, social, or financial survival is on the line.

But here's the thing: From an energetic or vibrational perspective, none of the dynamics you played out within the dramas of your early childhood experiences need to influence the vibration you offer the world today. We are the ones who keep the energy of our past very much alive by using past events to condemn, explain, or excuse who we now are or where we now stand. Most of us keep recycling the same behaviors, perspectives, thoughts, and actions that were hardwired into our nervous systems when we were children. If you've ever seen a child from a dysfunctional family playing with dolls, enacting scenarios in which one doll overpowers or bullies another and the other doll cowers in response, you know exactly what I'm talking about. These are the childish games that most adults are playing. We are re-enacting the dramas of our early childhood that would be done and dusted if not for the energy we keep feeding them. You do not need to do this.

You can instead realize that every interaction within the Triangle of Lack is being played out at your survival level of consciousness. This is the drama created by human beings who have forgotten where their true source of power, inspiration, and abundance comes from, and so we engage in the petty game of trying to steal, manipulate, and control the energy and abundance and inspiration from one another. Now, in the same way you no longer spend your days on merry-go-rounds but have graduated to more sophisticated creative endeavors, you can leave the Drama Triangle behind, have compassion for yourself as well as those who are still engaged within it, and seek your power, your energy, your inspiration, and your abundance from the stream of flow from which you were born and are inseparably a part of.

When you notice yourself or someone else acting out one of the parts within the Triangle of Lack, I invite you to look upon this in the same way you would look upon a person who believes they are drowning. A drowning person grasps at anything and everything that floats by, hoping it will help keep them afloat. If you saw a person flailing about because they believed they were drowning, you wouldn't get angry at them or take their flailing personally. You would understand that they're only behaving that way out of desperation, and you would throw them a mental life jacket in the form of compassion. This is where this entire conversation about childhood wounds, energetic imprints, and emotional triggers has been leading us—to compassion.

Compassion: The Key to Neutrality

Compassion is the key to stepping out of the energy of drama and lack and back into the energy of flow, because it is a high vibrational energy that has the power to soothe the raw nerves that trigger us into survival mode. Compassion is synonymous with understanding. When we understand our humanity, then we can have compassion for it.

I want to acknowledge that the word *compassion* doesn't resonate with everyone. If this is the case for you, please substitute it with the word *soothing* or *relief*. In applying the treatment of compassion, we're looking to create a little more space between the stimulus and our response, to offer ourselves and others the benefit of the doubt, and to be easy with ourselves—rather than doubling down on our tendency to criticize—when our primitive reactions are triggered. Personally, I equate the sensation of bathing myself in the energy of compassion to the feeling of crawling into a freshly made bed with a soft comforter and big comfy pillows after a long, hard day or the feeling of the big, deep sigh you release when the plane touches down safely after a turbulent or anxiety-ridden flight. It neutralizes all that chaotic survival energy and brings us back into equilibrium. It's this feeling of wrapping ourselves in a vibration of soothing relief that we're reaching for.

When we see someone acting out in rage, or manipulating, or trying to take care of everyone else as a way of soothing their own anxiety, compassion helps us recognize that, like someone who believes they are drowning, this person also feels threatened and powerless and is doing whatever they have instinctively learned how to do to try to feel better and get back into flow. When we view other people's behavior through the eyes of compassion, we don't judge it because we see that we have these same tendencies within ourselves. It's also essential to feel compassion for ourselves when we catch ourselves behaving in a way that is out of alignment.

When we have compassion for the still-wounded parts of ourselves—for our younger selves who experienced the fear, the abandonment, the desperation—we allow that repressed energy from the past to come up, and in that red-hot moment, we release ourselves from the vibrational patterns of our past. I am telling you this not as theory but from my own personal experience, hundreds and hundreds of times. For example, last summer I worked with a woman named Katie who had been trying for years to attract her ideal partner, but found herself enacting the same limiting patterns anytime she got close to someone. As soon as she'd meet a man who seemed like a fit, or who showed genuine interest in getting to know her better, Katie would get scared, withdraw, and then break off the connection before it ever had a chance to develop. As Katie shared her dating history with me, she did so with such harsh judgment and self-recrimination—as if it were her fault that she wasn't yet with the man of her dreams.

During our work together, Katie began to feel compassion for the wounded parts of herself that kept men at a distance, and she began to recognize that her patterns of avoidance were in place to try to keep her safe. Once she saw these tendencies as her ally rather than her enemy, she was able to stay in a more neutral and detached place. When getting close to a man triggered uncomfortable feelings, she acknowledged the sensations and centered herself back in the present moment, rather than react in real time to a memory from the past. Compassion allowed Katie to remember that today is different than yesterday, and to be more willing to discover where each day would take her. Six months after we began our coaching work, Katie announced that she was dating someone exclusively. And at the time of this writing, she and that someone are engaged to be married.

Katie's story is not unique; in my coaching work and healing events over the past two decades, I have seen people release the blocked and repressed energy that keeps them living as though they are Victims, Persecutors, or Rescuers and that manifests in their lives as financial debt and struggle, patterns of dysfunction in important relationships, physical pain or excess weight, and all types of other symptoms in their physical bodies.

In the appendix of this book, I teach you a variety of techniques to get back into flow, but I want you to understand that compassion is the first essential ingredient needed to effectively apply them all. Compassion is just an acknowledgment that there are places within us that are still reactive, that are still unconscious, that are still vibrating in harmony with the crazy dynamics of our early childhood or previous relationships—they feel split, separate, or not enough. It's an acknowledgment that there are still parts of us that don't yet know that we have other options and that we have within us the capacity to process discordant energy on the spot, rather than storing it in our bodies, numbing it with a substance, or dumping it onto others.

To apply the treatment of compassion when you find yourself in the middle of an uncomfortable situation or when someone comes at you with energy that doesn't feel good and your body understandably registers this energy as a threat to your well-being, take a moment to thank your survival instincts for making this known to you. No matter how far along the path of spiritual realization you may travel, your survival impulses are not going to go away, nor would you want them to. So simply acknowledge your built-in response to either fight, flee, freeze, or fawn, and take a moment to pause in compassion.

Taking a Pause

When life unfolds in a way that doesn't sit right with you, that brings up more resistance within you than it does flow, and all you can hear are those competing voices in your head urging you to act out from the wounded part of you and don the role of the Persecutor, the Victim, or the Rescuer, I invite you to acknowledge those tendencies and to take a pause instead. Become present to what is happening within you in this exact moment and breathe. Observe that even though your pulse may be racing, your emotions reeling, and your mind flooding you with thoughts such as *This shouldn't be happening*, you still have a choice as to which perspective you hold.

You can choose the perspective of lack, which will tell you that indeed something has gone very wrong and that it's your job to fix it. Then, with all the futility of an old man shaking his fist at the wind or shouting at the sky to stop the rain, you can attempt to control the flow of life and the behavior of other people, and you can compound your misery and your experience of lack in the process.

Or you can stop, become present in the moment, breathe, and send yourself some much-needed compassion for whatever predicament you find yourself in. You can remind yourself that you always have the free will to choose your actions, your words, your thoughts, your feelings, and your perspectives. Even when things around you appear to be falling apart, you still have the power to choose the perspective of abundance and flow, which will not only bring you instant relief but will cause you to look for and find the perfection of everything that's happening, even if it's not playing out even remotely as you had intended. Let me give you a quick example.

This past spring, Frederic and I flew to Colorado with our youngest son, Maxim, for his travel soccer team's weekend tournament. We flew out late on a Friday afternoon, and even though it was the middle of April, it was freezing cold in Colorado and there was snow on the ground when we arrived. When Maxim met up with his friends and teammates at the hotel and found the pool area covered in snow, the boys erupted in joy, throwing snowballs, giggling, running around, and having the time of their lives. When we woke up the next morning, even more fresh snow had fallen overnight, and we received the news that the morning game had been canceled. The boys were unfazed by this news, of course, too busy enjoying themselves in the smooth blanket of snow.

As some of the other parents lamented the "wasted trip" and others got on their phones to demand the field be cleared, Frederic and I opted for a perspective of flow. We chose to focus on watching our son play with his friends, experiencing the greatest joy either of us had ever seen him in. We focused on the crisp Colorado weather, such a stark and welcome contrast to the desert heat we had left behind. While Maxim played back at the hotel, Frederic and I used the time we would have spent on the soccer field to luxuriate over a long breakfast, just the two of us, where we talked and connected and reflected and appreciated and dreamed. Because we were open to perceiving the flow of energy that always is moving around and through us, we were able to take advantage of that rare blip in our busy schedules and make the most of that few-hour delay. By early that afternoon, the field had been cleared and the soccer tournament resumed. And instead of carrying the energy of frustration and blown expectations into the remainder of the weekend, Frederic and I felt truly grateful and blessed, both to have witnessed Maxim's joy and to have joined him in that high-flying vibration.

The more times you pause and practice mastering your own energy, despite whatever is going on around you, the more confident in that mastery you will become. Eventually you will come to realize that you really can handle other people's agitation because you have the ability to redirect and adapt the energy that arises within you in response to whatever they're throwing down. You'll come to truly understand that you are not just the flesh-and-blood bundle of nerves and automatic primitive urges that have been hardwired into your body; you are the stream of energy that inhabits your body. With practice, you begin to see that your thoughts and emotions are only energy, and you, my friend, are an energy receiver, a container, and a transmitter—a living and breathing energy processing plant. You were built to feel, accommodate release, and direct energy. You got this!

And so, when your fight, flight, freeze, or fawn instincts get triggered and your consciousness shrivels down to a tiny point where all you can see is what you appear to be lacking, or when your early conditioning is tempting you to wallow in *Woe is me*, or make others responsible for your pain, or distract yourself by soothing someone else's discomfort rather that dealing with your own—instead of jumping into one of those well-practiced roles, you can choose to be the one who compassionately observes this tendency. You can say to yourself, *Wow, my perception in this moment is that I am lacking something I need to survive, something I need to feel whole and complete, something I need to be happy. The human animal within me is telling me that if only I could numb myself from this feeling of fear, or if only I could change the other people around me, or if only I could prove to so-and-so that I really am a good person, then I would feel better; then I would be in flow.* In the same way you would soothe a child who is crying or an animal who is scared, you can look at your reactive self through compassionate eyes and realize nothing has gone wrong here. It's just the animalistic part of your consciousness, whose job it is to keep you safe, raising its head to evaluate the situation. You can give yourself the grace of understanding that of course your nervous system is reacting this way, given all that you have lived and the imprints that your life experiences have left on you. And you can compassionately thank this part of you for doing its job and acknowledge that there is a whole menu of other choices that are now available to you. Compassion is the frequency that allows you to take your wounded, scared, reactive self by the hand and walk it gently back to this present moment, where all your power lies.

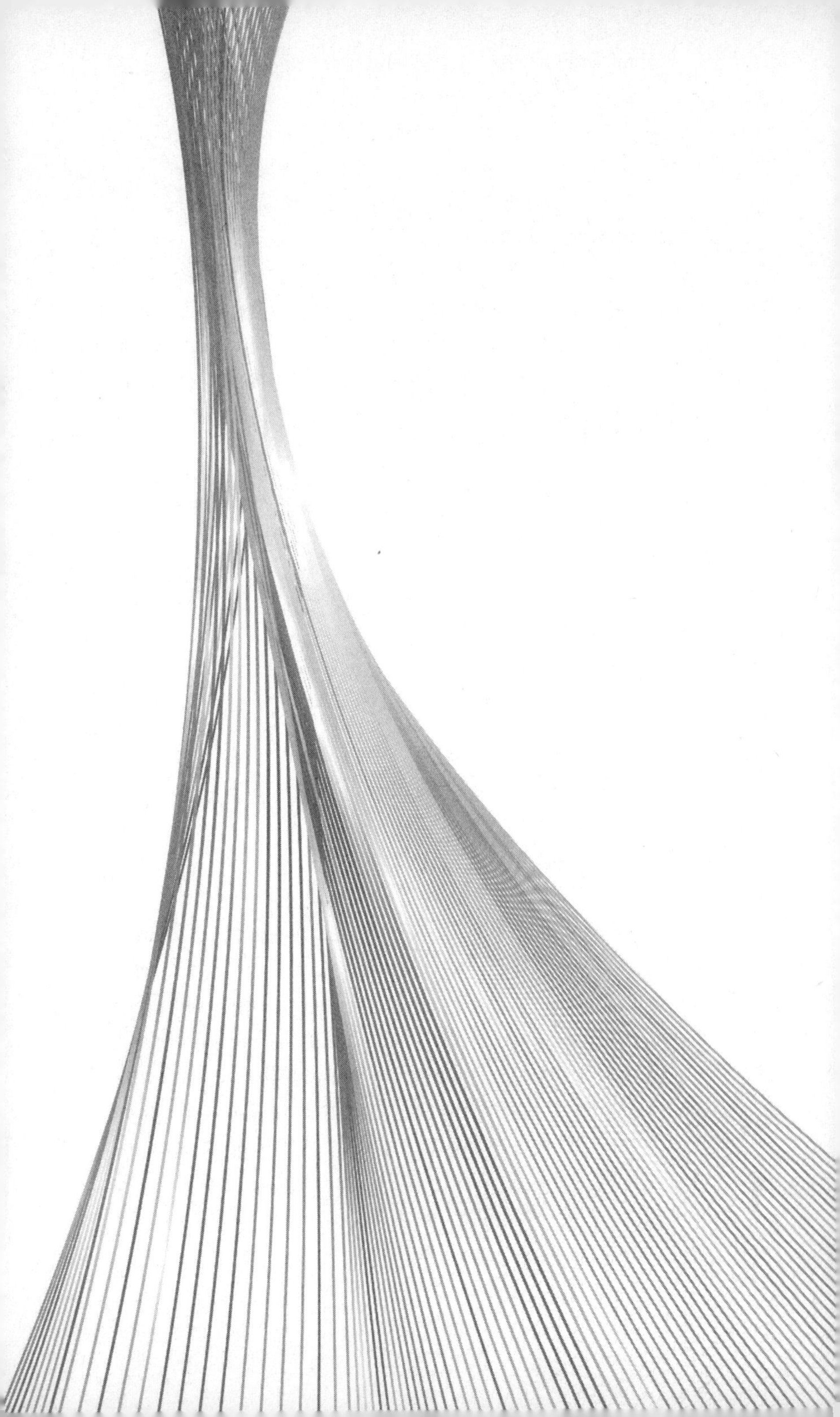

5

Contrast as an Invitation to Energy Mastery

It's time now to take our exploration of topics thus far—about the energetic nature of this universe; about the fact that we human beings are energy receivers, containers, and transmitters; and about the tendency we all have to store within us the energy of our unhealed and unprocessed emotional wounds—and apply this understanding to the places in life where the rubber hits the road, so to speak. I'm referring to those situations, circumstances, relationships, and events that appear to stand in direct opposition to our desires, that pinch us off from the energy flow that permeates this abundant universe when we focus on them, and that consequently cause us the greatest suffering. In this chapter as well as the appendix, I'm going to show you how to use any contrasting experience that is causing you pain or limitation as a powerful launching-off point to bring yourself back into the joyous, creative stream of flow and back into the life-giving inspiration you feel when you are aligned with your desires rather than doubting them. Let's begin with a reminder of the basic definition of *contrast*.

What Is Contrast?

The *Oxford English Dictionary* defines the word *contrast* as "the state of being strikingly different from something else in juxtaposition or close association." Since this is a book about flowing with the nonphysical energy that underlies every physical thing to align with and create the outcomes we desire, I am using the word *contrast* to refer to those moments in time when we experience something that is strikingly different than the experience of flow. As I mentioned earlier, I first learned about the universal principle of contrast from Abraham, as channeled by Esther Hicks, who describes it as the gap between what we desire and what we're currently experiencing.

Contrasting experiences can range from the overwhelming and extreme, such as losing a beloved person, possession, or dream, to relatively insignificant experiences, like being treated rudely by a salesperson or getting stuck in traffic. Some contrasting events are universally upsetting—things like death, conflict, heartbreak, and taxes—while others are highly individual and deeply personal, such as getting turned down for a job you feel you are perfect for. The reason that contrast shows up differently for each one of us is because each of us defines contrast according to our own unique and relative life experiences. For example, the COVID-19 pandemic was a source of stress and hardship for just about everyone, but healthcare and other essential workers whose livelihoods positioned them squarely on the front lines faced a disproportionate degree of trauma, hardship, and stress.

Contrast can manifest as something outside of you—like a project or relationship that is not unfolding as smoothly as you've imagined it—or it can manifest internally, as a bad mood or a feeling of having less inspiration, less enthusiasm, or less clarity than you would like. And contrast can come on slowly, as in the case of an intimate relationship that's become more tense, discordant, and miserable over many years, or it can come on quite suddenly, such as making the shocking discovery that your spouse is having an affair. The day I received the phone call that my sister, Terri, had died by suicide is an example of contrast that was both sudden and extreme. All these forms of contrast introduce a frequency of contradiction into our personal vibration that has the potential of knocking us out of flow state and back into survival mode. As I mentioned to you earlier in this book, I affectionately refer to the sudden onset of a contrasting experience as a "bushwhack."

Bushwhack: A Sudden Loss of Vibrational Altitude

A bushwhack is what you experience when a contrasting event triggers a pocket of discordant energy within you that abruptly interrupts your vibrational momentum. From big to small, like a plane that's cruising along and suddenly loses altitude or your device getting disconnected from Wi-Fi in the middle of a search, bushwhacks leave us unsettled and bewildered, until we regain our vibrational bearings, that is. Here are a few more everyday examples:

- You expect to travel for work or vacation with ease and your flight is canceled or delayed.

- You happily bounce into your favorite coffeehouse to get a drink and see someone you no longer speak to also grabbing a drink.

- You spend extra time getting ready for a special night out and your significant other criticizes your outfit.

- You approach your teenager with a heart full of love and eagerness to connect and they slam the door in your face.

- You're humming along feeling happy with the profitability of your business, then get hit with an unexpected fine or tax bill.

A bushwhack pulls the rug out from under us, so to speak, abruptly transporting us off the high-flying frequency of flow and back into a less desirable vibration that doesn't feel good.

Whether it's big or small and whether we're braced for it or not, a bushwhack takes us by surprise—our awareness of contrast begins with a disturbance in our chi, our energy body, which can sometimes be so subtle that only those of us who are really sensitive to energy will even register that something is off. Then, if that subtle discord is allowed to gain momentum, it will continue its further manifestation into our emotional body—our heart and solar plexus—where it has the potential to trigger an unhealed wound from our past. If the contrasting event does trigger an unhealed wound, it will reactivate all the associated energy that we've repressed around that event, which we will experience as if it's happening all over again, even though

Contrast as an Invitation to Energy Mastery

we are now in a new time and place. For example, it's fair to say that most of us would register a spouse criticizing our outfit as a contrasting or unwanted experience, but if you happened to grow up in a household or had experienced another relationship, friendship, or situation in the past where you were frequently belittled for your clothing choices, then for you, that criticism will cut a bit deeper. It's like if someone comes up and cheerfully claps you on the shoulder to say hello, but you have a sunburn or shoulder injury. Under normal circumstances that tap would probably feel good, but this time, you're perceiving it in a whole different way.

If our reaction to the contrasting event is allowed to gain even more traction, the discordant energy will then manifest in our mental body, causing us to search for both a cause and a solution for our disturbance. Our minds will scan the environment, looking for who or what is right and wrong in this situation, who or what is to blame for our discomfort, and what conditions we can manipulate in the outer world to feel better inside. In this fragmented state, we will then enact our familiar roles within the Triangle of Lack, which we discussed in the previous chapter. If the energy imbalance triggered by the contrasting situation continues to gain yet more momentum, it will eventually manifest in our physical body, first as tension and then as any number of symptoms and conditions that reflect our inner state of misalignment.

To summarize, contrast is what you experience when you're focused on something you don't want in any aspect of your life. It could be an external person, situation, or event, or it could be a state of being within yourself. And anytime you are faced with contrast, you have just two basic choices:

- **Choice A:** You can manifest your discomfort—which is to say, you can assume the role of Victim, Persecutor, or Rescuer and fight it, run from it, numb yourself to it, or try to people-please your way out of it. In making this choice, you are essentially allowing the external condition to dominate and merge with your inner vibration. This means when you encounter someone or something whose vibration is high, resonant, and clear, your vibration calibrates with it, and you feel happiness and a sense of flow. When you encounter someone or something whose energy is chaotic, depressed, or angry, your frequency takes that energy in, and you relinquish your state of happiness and flow for a lower, slower vibration. Incidentally—as maybe you have noticed—most of the world is opting for choice A.

- **Choice B:** Then there is the choice that this book is all about—to pause, breathe, and then flow. To use every situation—those that are high-flying as well as those that are filled with resistance—as an opportunity to master your energy and further clarify and strengthen your desired vibration, in the same way that intense pressure and high temperatures transform carbon into diamonds.

The way you choose to perceive and interpret each contrasting situation you encounter is what determines which choice you make.

It's Not the Event— It's the Meaning You Assign to It

You see, what spits us out of flow state and creates the energetic bushwhack within us is never just the contrasting event itself but what we make the event mean about ourselves. For example, the gut punch you feel upon discovering that a spouse has cheated is devastating, but this is not only because of a sex act that occurred between two people. The real bushwhack comes as a result of what you make that act mean about yourself. For example, *I'm not enough. He is going to leave me. I always fail in relationships. I'm unlovable. I'm too much work. The world is dangerous, and people are not to be trusted.* The interpretations we come up with in response to life's contrasts are endless in their variety, but here are some that have made the top ten list from the individuals I've worked with through the years. As you read through this list of limiting interpretations, see how many of them ring true for you:

- I don't deserve to be loved by others. I am unlovable.

- There is something wrong with me.

- It's my fault when people get upset.

- Other people's needs are more important than mine.

- If I have to ask for what I need from others, it means they don't really love me.

- If people knew who I really am, they would reject me.

- It's dangerous to express my feelings and needs directly.

- I must be perfect or others will abandon me.

- It's not safe to ask for help even when I need it.

- If I stay invisible and don't make waves, then I will be safe.

Once these interpretations and beliefs are formed within us—usually when we're very young, but sometimes later as well—they become part of our background operating system, so to speak, and we unconsciously filter everything that happens to us in the present through that particularly colored lens of the past. So, if the person who already had a belief that the world is a dangerous and unpredictable place gets laid off, that person will react entirely differently than the person whose interpretation of the world is that it's safe and generous and loving.

This is the phenomenon that *A Course in Miracles* (a spiritually-based program for inner peace) describes in lesson five when it suggests that "I am never upset for the reason I think." Our interpretation of a present-day experience transports our consciousness back to some earlier time during which we felt disrespected or unwelcomed or overwhelmed, and it's usually the reactivation of that lower, slower energy stream within us that sends our vibration plummeting—not the triggering event itself.

The Law of Attraction Amplifies Both Wanted and Unwanted

Most of us tense up against contrasting experiences big or small, believing that by railing against things unwanted, we can protect ourselves from them. Remember that this is a universe of energy that gathers and becomes more than it was before based on the similarity of frequency. I'm speaking again of the universal Law of Attraction, the metaphysical principle that states that what we focus on expands. When we tense up in resistance to an unwanted experience, we only extend an invitation for more resistance to manifest along our path. This may be sad, and at times it can certainly feel unfair, but it's still very true. When we permit unhealed and unprocessed toxic energy to remain within us, it's like we're walking around with a Kick Me sign taped to our back. We're unwittingly inviting the universe and all its variety of inhabitants and components to continue triggering our wound.

Have you experienced this firsthand? And have you ever wondered how it happens with such precision? Can anyone explain why the unthinking remark made by your best friend or your boss finds its way with laser-like accuracy to the exact place within your psyche that is the most wounded? It is because this is the Law of Attraction at work. That emotional wound is made up of energy—a vibrating, pulsating frequency of energy—that does not cease to attract similar frequencies to it even though you may have tried with everything you've got to push it out of your conscious awareness. This energy wants more than anything to be acknowledged, felt, mined for the wisdom it contains, appreciated, and then released. As Carl Jung explained in his highly acclaimed work *Memories, Dreams, Reflections,* "When an inner situation is not made conscious, it happens outside, as fate." In other words, life will continue triggering our unhealed energy until such time that we are finally willing to deal with it. This is why I say that when you are faced with a potentially bushwhacking contrasting experience, you really only have a few choices: Avoid dealing with the buildup of toxic energy within you and continue projecting your discord outward toward the people and situations that trigger it, turn the negative energy inward on yourself, or make what was previously unconscious conscious and take on the healing of your inner world like a true energy master.

Interpretation Equals Reality

Our interpretations are unbelievably powerful because once we reach a conclusion about what a situation means, we interact with that conclusion as though it's the truth. When my fifteen-year-old son leaves his dirty dish on the counter rather than putting it in the dishwasher as I have asked, I can interpret this as the harmless absent-mindedness of a fifteen-year-old boy whose attention is being pulled in dozens of other directions or I can interpret it as evidence that he is selfish, that he disrespects me, and that I am being mistreated. Which interpretation I choose will have a huge impact on the frequency of my personal vibration and therefore on the quality of the reality I'm creating, which includes the quality of my relationship with my son.

The meanings we assign to contrasting events—even those as seemingly small as the one described previously—become the overarching themes of the narratives we are writing, in every moment, about our lives. Are we unconsciously writing a story in which we, the main characters, are overworked, unappreciated, victimized by circumstances, and for whom nothing ever works out? Or are we crafting a narrative in which we are the hero or heroine, the energy master who uses contrast as a blessing that shows us where our own blocked energy is keeping us from basking in the flow of abundance that is all around us? Do we interpret each setback or troubling event as having hindered us, or do we see it as having empowered, strengthened, and benefited us by contributing to our clarity and our wisdom?

Each contrasting event that you encounter presents a golden opportunity to develop more of the qualities you will need to become the person you desire to be and create the life you deeply desire to live. Initially, we see only the pain and miss the purpose of these events, but that's only because we're not looking deeply enough or from a broad enough perspective.

For example, for someone whose heart's desire is to become a mother, a positive pregnancy test is seen as a tremendous blessing and a gift. To then discover ten weeks later that she's had a miscarriage is a devastating loss and perhaps even seen as a punishment or a curse. What I want you to understand is that both events are only pit stops along the very winding road of this woman's life. The positive pregnancy test confirmed and solidified her desire, and this strengthened commitment to motherhood will no doubt serve her and her child immensely. But what of the miscarriage? Did that event not also help strengthen within her other characteristics, such as detachment, faith, selflessness, and unconditional love, which will be every bit as essential to her desire to be a great mom?

Contrast is a gift because it offers us a crash course in shifting our energy, and sometimes the only way to get our attention is with a shocking revelation. We simply dig deeper, learn more, and access different skills and resources during times of hardship than we do in times of ease. To receive the gift of any contrasting experience, you have to allow yourself to thoughtfully unpack it and open yourself to the transformation it's trying to ignite within you.

One day while editing this book, I was inspired to Google the phrase *tipping point*, which is a term that gets thrown around quite a bit in the personal-growth space. The answer that came back surprised me: "A tipping point, from a chemical perspective, is a critical threshold where a small change in conditions can lead to a dramatic and irreversible shift in the system."

This is the value of contrast. An intense amount of pressure is needed to propel a rocket ship to break free from Earth's gravity. A caterpillar is subjected to all manner of internal and external pressures within its cocoon before it is ready to emerge as a butterfly. And human beings often need to allow the pressure of a contrasting situation to build to the point of absolute intolerance before we are finally ready to surrender and allow a new way of being to come into view.

So, it all comes down to the way you choose to perceive each contrasting event that manifests in your experience. Will you choose to make it mean that you've regressed, you've failed, you're not enough, you're broken, you're being punished, or you're doing a bad job of deliberately creating your life? Or will you choose to understand and interpret this contrast for the important role it's playing in helping you clarify your desire and flow the energy that creates worlds toward its realization?

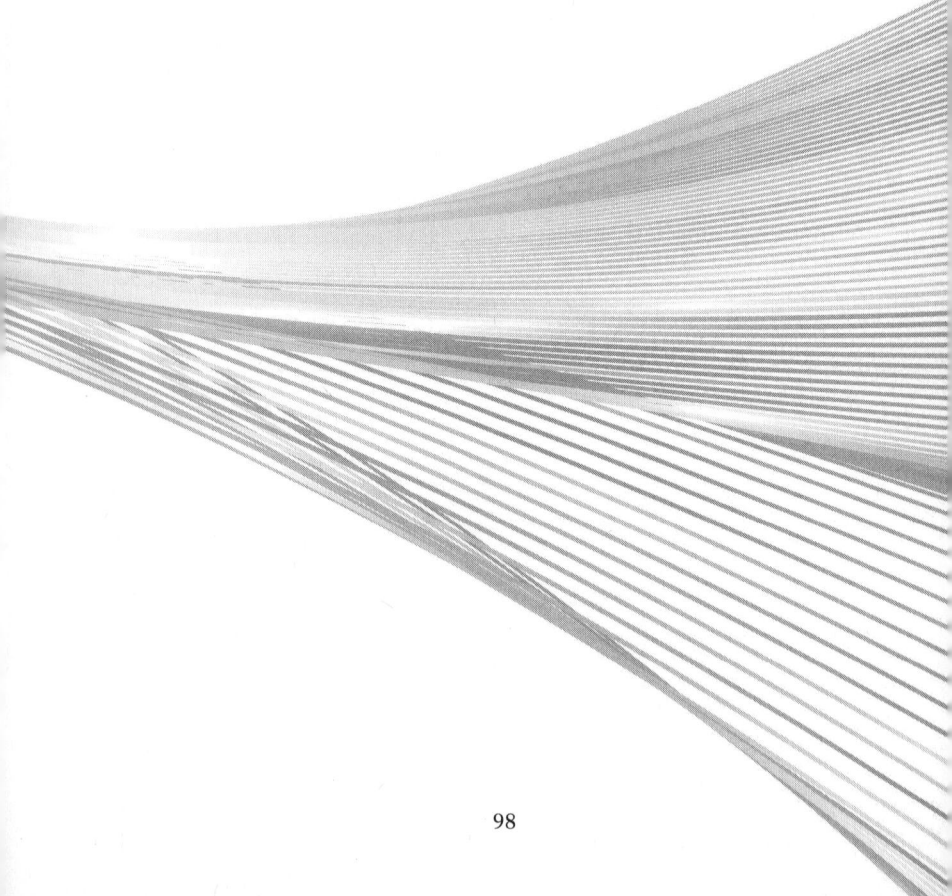

Contrast as Guidance

Pain is evidence that two vitally important things are happening simultaneously: First, you have a desire, and second, you're currently in a state of resistance to, rather than in a state of allowance of, that desire. It's easy to misinterpret uncomfortable emotions like frustration or fear as evidence that something has gone wrong, that something within your inner or outer world needs to be fixed or changed. I invite you to interpret them instead as guidance.

Your strong reaction to whatever contrasting event is currently unfolding is bringing your attention to the fact that this situation matters. What's unfolding here is important to you, and the rush of energy you're feeling inside yourself is letting you know that. If you've ever had a near miss in traffic, you know that contrast has the power to wake us out of the trance of humdrum life, flooding every cell of our bodies with an instant reminder of what really matters. Less important priorities drop away, and we're left in a state of absolute clarity about what's truly important.

Contrast focuses our energy and makes us crystal clear about what we want—by making us crystal clear about what we don't want. Any uncomfortable feelings we have in the face of that realization are just an indication of resistance. They're letting us know that, in this moment at least, we are more aligned with the problem than we are with the solution; we're more aligned with asking the question than we are with receiving the answer.

As a wise creator, surely you can appreciate this guidance. How else would you know if you are in or out of alignment? The discomfort we feel during times of contrast is not about the event itself. It's about the constriction of energy inside of us. And we can either continue suppressing this energy or projecting outward, as in fits of road rage or emotional tantrums, or we can take the opportunity to purify our energy body and release the resistance from within.

What I hope this book has shown you is that you do not have to wait until your resistance reaches an intolerable crescendo—or until your fight, flight, freeze or fawn tendencies have wound you into a state of exhaustion—to begin leaning more toward the solution than the problem. I hope it has shown you that everything on planet Earth operates under the principle of duality. Clarity exists on the other side of confusion, ease on the other side of tension. Every time you feel constriction, it's only because there is a greater expansion that is calling you toward it. If in the middle of your resistance you can remember that the pressure that's building within you is the exact force that will help to catapult you into the next level of consciousness, and if you can soothe yourself into cooperating with that process instead of fighting against it, then this book will have served its purpose. Your resistance is the rocket fuel that helps break you free from the gravitational force of whatever plateau you've been stuck in. You don't need to hang out in that discomfort indefinitely.

In the appendix that follows, I guide you through specific energy mastery processes that you can apply anytime your energy has tipped from a state of flow into a state of resistance. Your inner guidance, in all its brilliance, is what will let you know this tip has occurred. Sometimes you'll experience the contrast as a physical pain or blockage. Other times it will manifest as a lack of inspiration, a persistently bad mood, or a stream of negative thoughts moving with so much momentum that you feel you have no control of them. These energy mastery processes will show you exactly how to release that unwanted momentum so you can find neutrality, compassion, relief, clarity, and the return of flow.

Before we move forward, I want to emphasize that the most important thing you can bring to these energy mastery processes is a commitment that when contrast throws you off, physically, emotionally, mentally, or energetically, you will seek first and foremost to regain your inner alignment. You can't heal what you don't own, so accepting that the imbalance begins with you has to be your primary commitment. The techniques themselves are simply the means that you employ to release resistance and regain your inner balance. The awareness that this is an inside job, period, is what's most important.

There Will Always Be Contrast

The fact is this: Contrast isn't going anywhere. It's part and parcel of our human experience, so we might as well learn to embrace and learn from it rather than squander our energies trying to conquer or avoid it. So, when we find ourselves writhing in discomfort because what we want is taking too long or we're experiencing a setback or a health challenge, we have to take a step back and ask ourselves, *What ideal am I holding myself to?* If we're holding the ideal that life should always be peaceful or that our desires should unfold effortlessly and without any struggle whatsoever, we are setting ourselves up for continual stress. Life is a series of highs and lows, and the lows are the only thing that give the highs any meaning. I know this may sound cliché, so I'm urging you to really think about what I'm saying here.

How engaging would a video game be if there was no chance of losing points or having to start over from the beginning? How satisfying would it be to go to a lunch buffet that offered only one type of food—even if it was your favorite food in the entire world? Or what if every time you attempted to land a basketball in the hoop, you never missed a shot?

What if every single ball, no matter where you were standing on the court, landed in the basketball hoop with a resounding *swish*? If you never missed a shot, would the game have any meaning or be any fun at all?

What if the radio played only one genre of music? Or if music itself was made up of only harmonic tones with no discordant notes? It's only in the presence of the discord that we can distinguish and appreciate the harmony. *This* is the value of contrast. You may have some notion that you want your life to be only smooth sailing, but without some waves, without some variance in the vibration, everything you experience would be monotone and mind-numbingly uninteresting. Does this make sense?

In life, you seek out the roller coaster, the scary movie, the twist-filled dramatic novel . . . why? Because you know that there is a depth and richness of experience that only becomes possible in the presence of contrast. There would be no joy in accomplishment without the exertion of effort, no release in having a good cry if not for the previous buildup of emotional tension. You crave moments of connection and peace only because you have known moments of pain and discord, and when things get too peaceful, you want more passion and adventure, do you not?

As a wise creator, you understand this universal principle that contrast is part of our human experience, and you use this knowledge to your advantage. You acknowledge that of course you are going to feel down sometimes because life wouldn't be life if it were not for both the ups and the downs. Of course you're going to feel lost or unsure sometimes, and without that contrast, you would never be able to appreciate—or even recognize—how good it feels to be found. Activating the Flow Factor in your life does not mean that everything goes your way all the time. It means that you have a built-in psychological buffer for contrast so that life's inevitable bumps in the road don't knock you off into the bushes, aka back into victim consciousness and survival mode.

As deliberate creators, we simply must develop a relationship with contrast, because as surely as the sun rises and sets, life's highs and lows are not going anywhere. Unwanted things are going to happen. No amount of knowledge or money or cleverness can prevent that. But the point is, just because something unwanted is playing out in your experience doesn't mean you're a bad creator or that you've done something wrong. It only means that life is made up of ups and downs, of darkness and light, of having and not having. So, when something wanted fades away and you feel the pain of its absence, you know the tide will come in again because that's the inevitable cycle of life. There will always be another wave.

CONCLUSION

I have been a teacher of energy mastery for over twenty-five years, and in that time, I've made some pretty big promises to those like you who find their way to my message. For example, it is my promise that you were born to know yourself as a boundless spirit incarnated into a finite human body and to live a life of absolute joy and abundance. You were designed to manifest your dreams; to create financial and material prosperity; to enjoy loving and fulfilling relationships; to experience balance, strength, and pleasure in your physical body; to live your passion and purpose through your career or creative self-expression; and to continue to expand your consciousness to own more and more of your spiritual power while you are here in a manifested form. You were born with these desires in your heart, and you came here to realize them all.

Often when I am coaching someone who has come up against a limitation that's blocking them from realizing one of these heartfelt desires, they will say something to the effect of *Maybe I am not supposed to have this*. "Maybe I'm not supposed to start my own business," they say. "Maybe I'm not meant to have that kind of money or that level of success," or "Maybe I was never supposed to be a mom." This, my friends, is what it sounds like when we run up against a limitation that we resist, rather than flow with and around and through. Our resistance then stifles the natural bubbling up of our own desires, blocks our connection with the universal flow of energy that we were born to have unlimited access to, and leaves us feeling despondent, lifeless, and resigned.

What I say to these coaching clients, and what I'm saying to you now, is that there is no such thing as "supposed to." There is no all-powerful deity sitting on a cloud somewhere dictating what you can or cannot do, be, or have. Free will is the guiding principle that grants each person the power to shape their own destiny. This is a universe of unending abundance, but the door to allowing or disallowing its flow lies within you and you alone. How much you allow yourself to receive comes down to this: Have you developed the mastery to keep your physical, emotional, mental, and energy bodies open and receptive in the face of life's diversity, or do parts of you still reflexively shut down, blocking the flow of all that you could be choosing instead?

In those moments when contrasting experiences are piling up all around you and you're gripped by your primitive instincts to survive at all costs, are you willing to intentionally expand your focus and shift your consciousness from fear back to flow? Are you willing to see this moment as perfect, to believe that this universe is friendly? Are you willing to inch your way up your internal ladder of consciousness, from despair and powerlessness to empowerment and flow?

Please remember that you are an energetic being. In your very bones, in your electrical circuitry, you know how to find flow. You have had many moments of it, particularly when you were a young kid. You may have been raised in a massively dysfunctional household or one in which there was poverty or addiction all around you,

Conclusion

but you absolutely had those moments—maybe playing out in a field near your home or maybe in the presence of a connected grandparent or godparent or friend—when you knew in every cell of your being that all is well, that you are special, and that most certainly the chaos manifesting around you is not all there is to life.

It has been my goal throughout this book to show you some paths for returning to that original understanding that resonates deep in your bones. The path is not the same for everyone and will be different at different times in your life and in different seasons and circumstances. If you take to heart the principles that have been outlined here, I know these principles will act as signposts that you can use to guide you on your way. As the Council says, "You are infinitely loved and supported, and since the flow is always with you, use it to create what you desire."

APPENDIX

Energy Mastery Processes to Move from Resistance to Flow

Throughout this book, I've guided you along an in-depth exploration of flow: what it is, from where it originates, and what gets in the way of our experience of it. In this section are sixteen distinct energy mastery processes that will support you in reconnecting with the Flow Factor anytime you find yourself unable to access the clarity, abundance, and well-being that you desire and deserve to experience in your life.

The processes outlined in this section are designed for you to experience directly. As I learned from one of my earlier teachers, Abraham-Hicks, "Words don't teach. Only experience teaches." Your mind may comprehend all that you have read up to this point, but it's through working with these energy mastery processes that you'll integrate this understanding into a practical, moment-to-moment awareness of what it takes to shift your consciousness. This section puts everything into place so you can discover firsthand the clarity that is born from contrast and experience sacred transformation in your life.

I've included this appendix of processes so that you will have them for easy reference; however, to truly get the most out of these exercises, you'll want to listen to them passively, with your eyes closed and with your complete attention focused upon your own breathing and on the sensations that arise in your body and mind as you move through each one. If you'd like me to guide you through a complete meditation of any or all of the energy mastery processes described here so that all you will need to do is listen and experience their benefits, please visit theflowfactorbook.com to access the full library.

What's Included in This Appendix

This appendix is organized into four sections: The first section, titled "Energy Mastery Processes for Releasing Mental Resistance and Increasing Flow," contains processes that will support you in releasing resistance in the realm of your thoughts and mental outlook. The exercises outlined in the second section, titled "Energy Mastery Processes for Releasing Emotional Resistance and Increasing Flow," will support you in neutralizing the momentum of uncomfortable emotions. The third section, titled "Energy Mastery Processes for Releasing Physical Resistance and Increasing Flow," contains exercises that will guide you toward soothing relief when your physical body is on high alert and manifesting symptoms of survival mode rather than flow. The processes included in the final section, titled "Energy Mastery Processes for

Increasing Spiritual Flow," will be most beneficial when you're already in a neutral place and are seeking to fine-tune your vibration and further enhance your connection with universal intelligence and inspiration.

The purpose of each of these exercises is to show you how to increase your experience of the presence of flow, either by helping you to soften the resistance that may be obstructing your present ability to perceive it or by helping you to transcend your everyday awareness of human concerns so you can more easily access the realm of the divine. As such, you'll notice that the conscious invoking of the energy of compassion is a recurrent theme in many of these processes.

How to Use This Appendix

There are two ways to use the energy mastery processes in this section. The first is to simply read through the list of processes as you would a restaurant menu and select the one that most appeals to your current physical, mental, emotional, or spiritual state. The second way to utilize these processes is to consciously call into your awareness a specific outcome that you desire to create in your life that is not flowing with the clarity or speed that you would like, and then use the quick journaling exercise immediately following to help you determine whether your resistance resides primarily in the mental, emotional, or physical realm. Once you have greater clarity about the nature of your resistance, you can then turn to that section and choose from one of the four processes offered for restoring flow in that specific aspect of consciousness. If, after completing the journaling exercise, you discover that it's not the presence of resistance but rather an absence of clarity, inspiration, or faith that is blocking your experience of flow, turn to the fourth process section and choose from one of the four energy mastery exercises provided for increasing spiritual flow.

If you choose this latter option, please take a moment to get settled somewhere where you are unlikely to be disturbed, then grab a pen or a pencil and some paper to write on (and yes, I encourage you to go old-school and use the physical stuff instead of a computer or iPad).

A Quick Journaling Exercise for Clarity

Begin by considering what, specifically, you would like to create in yourself or in your life at this moment in time. In other words, if you had the power to shift just one thing in either your inner or outer world, what would you like that to be?

This could be something immediate, such as feeling greater comfort, ease, satisfaction, or happiness within yourself, or maybe it's about manifesting something you do not yet have, such as a new relationship or a job promotion.

This is not a time to criticize, judge, or analyze your desires nor to doubt or dismiss your heartfelt dreams. It's a time to express your flow. So please give yourself permission to dream without limitations about what you want and then journal your answers to the following questions:

1. What do you want?

2. Why do you want it?

3. How do you want to feel?

Appendix

Now, as you contemplate these questions, notice at which level of your being you experience the greatest opposition to these desires. Is it at the level of your mind? That is to say, when you contemplate having what you want, are you simultaneously aware of opposing thoughts, concerns, constraints, problems, or limitations? Or is your mental space cluttered or confused because you're considering too many other perspectives other than the one that you desire? If this is the case, begin with one of the processes listed in the section titled "Energy Mastery Processes for Releasing Mental Resistance and Increasing Flow."

When you contemplate your desire, does your resistance to it manifest primarily as a bad-feeling emotion, such as fear, self-doubt, frustration, loneliness, or heartbreak? Do you feel stressed out, fearful, discouraged, hopeless, or ill at ease? If so, begin with one of the exercises listed under the section titled "Energy Mastery Processes for Releasing Emotional Resistance and Increasing Flow."

If contemplating the object of your desire primarily evokes physical discomfort—such as muscle tension, headache, or another physical symptom such as insomnia or digestive issues—consider starting with one of the processes listed under the category called "Energy Mastery Processes for Releasing Physical Resistance and Increasing Flow."

And finally, if you do not experience resistance in response to these questions, but rather an absence of inspiration, connection, or clarity, consider beginning with one of the processes listed in "Energy Mastery Processes for Increasing Spiritual Flow."

You can return to this journaling exercise anytime you need to check in with yourself.

Appendix

Section 1: Energy Mastery Processes for Releasing Mental Resistance and Increasing Flow

PROCESS 1: SOOTHING THE REACTIVE MIND

1. Whenever you notice that your mind is reacting negatively to someone or something—whether it's something that's happening now, something that happened in the past, or something that may or may not happen in the future—use this as your cue that your reactivity is coming from a limiting perspective or belief, and take a moment to identify the specific thought within your mind that is triggering the reactivity. For example, *I spent all day doing something that didn't meet my supervisor's standards. I should already be done with this by now.* Notice the momentum of that negative or disempowering thought, and then tell yourself, *Take it easy. It's going to be fine. I'm okay. All is well.* Take a breath in and out.

2. Imagine opening the back of your head, where your skull and neck come together to form a divot, and allow all the energy of that reactivity to release out of the back of your brain. Visualize that, like turning on a faucet, you are opening that area just by focusing on it opening. Releasing this area will allow the energy of the limbic and nervous systems to calm down so that you can find a better-feeling thought. The flow of energy through your entire mental body will come back online, and you will no longer be stuck in the fight, flight, fawn, or freeze mode but will be back in a state of flow within your mental body.

Appendix

PROCESS 2: TENDING TO SPLIT ENERGY

As we discussed in chapter 2, split energy feels like having a foot in two different boats that are moving in different directions. You feel split. You want love, but you also don't want to get hurt. You want to create success, *but* you're afraid of failing so you procrastinate. We tend to hear *but* anytime we're in split energy. It can happen in the smallest moment of any day: *I want to get along with this person, but they can be so rude.* In fact, paying attention to the words you habitually use is one of the fastest ways to recognize when you are perpetuating a vibration of split energy within you. To understand more about how changing the words you speak can change your life, please visit watchyourwords.com. To tend to your split energy, do the following:

1. Imagine that you have one foot in one boat and another foot in a second boat, and each represents a competing thought or desire. *I want this, but* . . . As these thoughts are moving away from one other, they are causing you to feel stuck because you are not flowing all your energy in a single unified direction. Acknowledge this predicament.

2. Take out a piece of paper and on the left side of the page, write down what the conflicting thoughts are so that you can become aware of them. For example: *I know what I want, but it is taking so long that I am starting to doubt it will ever happen.*

3. On the right side of the page, write down what you do want, and what you want to believe about this aspect of your life. For example, *I want to feel loved and be in a connected relationship*, or *I want to be financially free*.

4. As you look objectively at these two streams of thoughts, ask yourself which stream you want to continue to flow your powerful creative energy toward. Make that choice and decide, *I want to think thoughts of love and not doubt,* or *I want to feel what it feels like now to have financial flow instead of being in debt.*

5. Replace the thoughts that don't feel good with better-feeling thoughts. For example, *Even though finding love has taken me longer than I anticipated, I am open and willing to receive,* or *Even though I struggled with money in the past, I now claim my financial freedom.* Then imagine you are taking your foot out of the boat that you no longer want to travel in and firmly placing both feet in the same boat.

6. Lastly, affirm to yourself, *Even though I had split energy on this topic in the past, I now fully flow and focus all of my creative energy on what I do want. What I want is _____.* Name it and claim it.

PROCESS 3: MOVING FROM FEAR OF LACK TO FAITH IN ABUNDANCE

1. **Become aware:** Anytime you are fearing that you don't have enough or that you will not have what you want in the future, it is because you are focusing on lack. Remember that lack *always* feels bad. So, the first step in shifting from a mindset of lack to one of abundance is to become aware of the lack-based thought that is causing the fear.

2. **Recognize the cause:** What thought of scarcity or lack is creating that fear? It will always be a perception or belief of "not enough." For example, *More is better, and I don't have that amount right now. I will need more, and I don't see how I can get more,* or *I just can't change the situation. Nothing I do can make it better.*

3. **Expand your awareness:** Acknowledge that the energy of flow, your source of all that is good, is with you now, and then become aware that you are responsible for creating your life and, therefore, for transforming any situation. Also become aware that if the experience of lack exists, the experience of abundance also exists here and now within this universe of polarity. Acknowledging both your personal responsibility and the duality of all things, ask yourself, *If I looked at this situation through the lens of abundance, what would I see? How could I perceive this situation in a way that feels good?* For example, *Everything has always worked out for me in the past, I always have options,* or *I'm divinely loved and cared for.*

4. **Open your third eye:** Open your third eye to the energy that you *do* want. The third eye is what the Council calls your Faith Portal, and it's located between your eyebrows. Imagine that the soothing frequency of faith is flowing into your third eye. Faith is the most important superpower that we have as humans. When you are focusing on the faith of what you do want, you move into the faith of fulfillment and abundance. You are either focused on the doubt of having it, the fear of it not coming, or the fulfillment of it. This choice is yours, as you are the only one inside your own mind and

the only one engaging in your thoughts. Make your choice now. Which do you choose?

5. **Visualize your desire:** Imagine what you desire to have. If what you desire were already a part of your experience, what would that look like? Fill this image out with as much color, texture, and detail as you can. When you see any other images of "not enough" that trigger fear, switch the channel in your mind like you would change the channel on the television. If you don't like the movie that is running in your mind, change it—put on the movie that uplifts and inspires you. Feel the energy of the contentment and fulfillment from having realized that desire here with you now. Bask in that vibration.

PROCESS 4: SLOWING THE RESISTANCE TO UNWANTED THOUGHTS

This is one of my favorite practices. Whenever I notice that I am having a thought that is gaining momentum, doesn't feel good, and isn't leading me in a direction that I want to go, I will take my hand and imagine that I am karate chopping the thought and with it, dissolving all the energetic momentum of that thought. Hi-ya! This action will create an energetic disconnection and give you the presence and freedom to be able to choose your thoughts deliberately.

1. Become aware of a resistant, bad-feeling, or unwanted thought. For example, *Oh no, what if my son gets hurt.*

2. Take your hand and cut that thought. *Hi-ya!*

3. Give yourself a nice flow of light energy into space you've just opened up in your mind.

4. Then choose a better, more empowering thought that more closely reflects what you *do* want. As you formulate this thought, feel your mental energy begin to flow toward the reality you desire to create. For example, *I see my son in full happiness and well-being, enjoying his experience.*

5. Visualize just for one minute the fulfillment of this desire.

Section 2: Energy Mastery Processes for Releasing Emotional Resistance and Increasing Flow

PROCESS 1: THE EMOTIONAL RELEASE PROCESS— NINETY SECONDS TO FREEDOM

1. Close your eyes and focus all your attention on your lower belly, placing a hand there and tightening the muscles under it.

2. Here you will feel a pulse or a rhythm. This is the seat of your emotional body, where you will stay focused throughout this process. Even though you may feel the unwanted emotion in other parts of your body and your mind may get involved, stay focused on your belly and allow yourself to ride that energy wave until the energy dissipates. There is no need to force anything or to try to make this process happen faster. It takes approximately ninety seconds to process a wave of emotions. If it is something slight, it might be a one-and-done situation. If you're processing an emotion that

Appendix

you have a deeper attachment to, such as the loss of someone you love, the waves of grief may take repeated rounds of ninety-second increments to pass through. Allow the process to unfold however it unfolds.

3. Imagine that you are a surfer in the ocean, waiting for a wave to come. The surfer is actively waiting for that momentum of the next wave. While you are focused on your lower belly and contracting the muscles, let yourself actively wait for the next wave of emotions. Let yourself feel whatever you are feeling.

4. Be aware that your emotions affect your entire body, so it's perfectly natural to feel the emotions in your heart center, in your throat, or in other parts of your body. Allow whatever is happening to be perfectly okay.

5. Wherever you are feeling the emotions in your body, remember that the lower belly is the first point where the emotions hit and will be the last point where the emotions release. So, when you feel it in a different part, focus on the belly and imagine that it is draining from the other parts where you feel it and back into your belly, your emotional center, where you can process it fully.

6. After the waves of emotion have released, allow yourself to imagine that you are standing under a waterfall of light and that this light is entering though the crown of your head at your seventh chakra, or your spiritual center. Let this light energy pour through your entire mind, your body, and your emotions. Notice the relief and the release. Now choose what and how you desire to feel.

7. Declare what you do want to feel. For example, *I want to feel free*, or *I want to feel at peace*. Imagine that the energy of your choosing is filling you up from the inside out.

PROCESS 2: SOOTHING HYPERSENSITIVITY AND REACTIVITY

1. To soothe something that you are hypersensitive and reactive to, begin by completing the ninety-second process described in the first exercise of this section.

2. Then ask yourself, *Which button, imprint, or little-t trauma was just ignited?* For example, *Am I feeling rejected or abandoned? Do I feel the need to protect or to defend my position?*

3. Allow yourself to review the situation that triggered the reactivity within you; then ask yourself, *What evidence do I have that this is not always the case and that it is just a single incident right now that has caused me to feel activated?* For example, if your partner falls short of your expectation in one exchange, you may think, *My partner does show me that he is there for me when he hugs me or comes home each night.* Take a deep breath into your lower belly.

Appendix

4. Ask yourself, *Am I in fight, flight, fawn, or freeze right now?* As you receive the answer, acknowledge it, then imagine that the energy center at the back of your head is opening. Allow any unnecessary survival instinct energy to drain out of your mind and out of the places in your body where you feel the imprint has been stored.

5. Ask yourself, *Is the thought, belief, or perspective that I reacted to something that I want to continue to feel and be sensitive and reactive to?*

6. If the answer is no, then ask yourself, *What other perspective could I adopt about myself, this person, or this situation?*

7. Choose to declare what you want to feel. For example, *I am safe. I am loved. I am supported by Source and the Divine Self. All is well.*

PROCESS 3: FILLING YOUR CUP—RECOVERING YOUR EMOTIONAL ENERGY AND VITALITY

1. When you find yourself in a moment of feeling not good or not as good as you would like to feel, do the ninety-second process described earlier in this section to release whatever is already being stored in your energy container.

2. Now that you are empty, allow yourself to fill up with the energy of light and compassion, which is soothing and replenishing.

3. Next, allow yourself to choose how you *do* want to feel in this moment. For example, *I want to feel joyful, loved, and free.*

Yes, you can create your own personal energy vibration by choosing a few emotions at a time, such as joyful, successful, happy, fun.

4. Now imagine that your energy container (your mind, body, emotions, and your energy body all around, above, below, outside, and inside of you) is filled with that frequency and those emotions. Feel that you have just moved into a bubble of this energy and you are now experiencing the emotion you desire.

PROCESS 4: COMPASSION BATH

1. Whenever you notice you're focused on something that doesn't feel good and you want to move out of that emotion, allow yourself to close your eyes.

2. Imagine that you are standing in the middle of a beautiful bubble of light. Five feet above you, below you, in front of you, behind you, and the entire space within and around you—everywhere is filled with glittering, shimmering love and light, with the frequency of compassion.

3. As you continue to focus on the presence of this light, acknowledge that you are now taking in and breathing in compassion itself. This is the energy of a compassion bath. Imagine slipping into a warm bath of compassionate energy; your body, your mind, your energy field, and every cell of your body is soaking in the light, bubbling energy of compassion. Continue to feel the energy of compassion moving from your physical body to your mental body to your emotional body, centered in your lower belly, then

expanding into your spiritual body or aura. Feel yourself surrounded by the frequency of compassion, which soaks into every cell of your body and radiates into your energetic field.

4. If you can, fill up your bathtub with warm water and declare with your intention that this water holds the frequency of compassion, which is soothing and comforting. Use a bath bomb or bubbles that feel comforting to you and soak in this energy bath until you feel relaxed and complete. There are even shower bombs now, and it can be just as soothing to stand under running water.

Section 3: Energy Mastery Processes for Releasing Physical Resistance and Increasing Flow

PROCESS 1: RELAXING YOUR BODY'S FIGHT RESPONSE—RELEASING ANGER AND RAGE

When we meet anger with judgment or allow shame or inhibition to suppress our body's fight response, we block the natural pathways that allow for its easy release. To mobilize this repressed energy, release the physical manifestations of anger and rage, and relax your body's fight response, physical cathartic movement is the tool of choice. While there are many methods for discharging the energy of stored or repressed anger (I list several in this process), I find the following to deliver the most satisfying release:

Appendix

1. Grab a carton of eggs and go out somewhere in nature, into the desert, the woods, a local park, or your own backyard.

2. Begin by taking some deep breaths, placing your awareness within and around your belly, and allowing yourself to connect with and feel the physical surge of anger throughout your body, particularly in and around your belly and your limbs.

3. Take one egg out of the carton, hold it near your belly, and imagine that all of the anger coursing through your body is being channeled into that egg. Allow your breath and vocalization to support you in this process. Take as long as you need to feel ready, and when you internally sense that your anger has been transferred into the egg, deliberately throw the egg with an audible sound, allowing yourself to feel the release of physical tension and fight energy as you do so.

4. Continue to process your anger by throwing the eggs until you feel that the fight energy has released out of you. As it mobilizes and leaves your body, you may feel a slight warmth, buzzing, or tingling sensation.

5. After you have released the lower-level energy, spend a few moments welcoming in the healing, soft energy of compassion. It is important to fill yourself up with the new, desired vibration of compassion and continue to flow with this energy after you have released the unwanted energy of anger; otherwise you will entrain with the old energy.

If throwing eggs does not seem practical to you or otherwise doesn't appeal to you, here are some other options:

Appendix

- Go for a brisk walk or spend fifteen minutes on a cardio machine at the gym.

- Dance freely to loud music, allowing your body to move at will.

- Punch your mattress with your fists while screaming into a pillow.

- Use a plastic whiffle bat to hit a mattress or the soft cushion of a chair.

- Write down all the things you are angry about on separate pieces of paper then crumple or tear the pieces of paper up.

- Schedule a session at a rage room—designed for the purpose of breaking and smashing things—if one is available nearby.

- Stay seated in a chair and bounce up and down deliberately while moving your arms and vocalizing.

Whatever method you choose for releasing the energy of anger and rage, please keep these two important principles in mind:

1. Be mindful of your safety and the safety of others before, during, and after this process. This includes communicating in advance to family members or roommates who may overhear you during this process, ensuring that the space you're in is free from dangerous objects before you begin, and cleaning up any materials left behind (such as eggshells or pieces of paper) after you are finished.

Appendix

2. It's important to remember that this process isn't just about moving your body; it's about mobilizing and releasing stored energy. Even if your capacity for physical movement is limited, you can use whatever range of motion you have to facilitate the movement of energy. Adapt this process to the needs of your body.

PROCESS 2: RELAXING YOUR BODY'S FLIGHT RESPONSE—SOOTHING FEAR AND ANXIETY

Fear and anxiety almost always manifest in our physical bodies as rapid or shallow breathing—or, in times of acute stress, as a temporary cessation of breath altogether. For this reason, conscious breathing is one of the fastest and most effective ways to restore flow when your body is gripped by the flight response.

1. Begin by finding a comfortable seat somewhere quiet where you are unlikely to be disturbed. Dedicate the next several minutes to releasing the physical manifestations of fear and anxiety from your physical body, so you can easily return to your natural state of flow.

2. Close your eyes and consciously begin to lengthen both your inhale and your exhale. Give yourself a few moments to settle in and then begin to follow the length of each one of your breaths. Breathe in slowly and deeply for a count of seven. At the top of your inhale, hold your breath for seven counts. Breathe out slowly and completely for a count of seven. At the end of your exhale, hold your breath for a count of seven, then repeat.

3. As you continue repeating this breathing pattern, notice that it resembles a square or a box, with the four sides of the box corresponding to the four phases of your breath. If it helps, you can follow your process visually by tracing the box's outline in your mind.

4. Continue this process for several minutes, noticing that as your physical body settles and your nervous system is soothed and calmed, your emotional body follows suit.

PROCESS 3: RELEASING YOUR BODY'S FREEZE RESPONSE—SOOTHING INDECISION AND ESCAPISM

The wisdom of this energy mastery process taps into the power that you make available to yourself when you simply—and consciously—allow yourself to be where you are, rather than force yourself to move into action before you're ready. When you honor rather than resist your natural freeze instinct, you can more easily decipher what's triggering the resistance within you in the first place. Then when you do decide to move into action, you can do so from a state of alignment and clarity.

1. Begin by making the decision to honor your body's wise instinct to hide or camouflage itself in the face of some perceived danger and find a place that feels safe and protective. Respect whatever place your instinct directs you toward,

whether that's going into your car, a closet, the bathroom, or even curling up under the covers in your bed. The goal here is to provide the part of you that feels small and unresourceful with the sensation of comfort and safety, so please give that to yourself without judgment, in whatever way feels just right.

2. Once you feel settled and out of sight, reassure yourself that it's okay to feel however you're feeling right now and that there is no need to rush to feel any different. Whatever words come up for you that describe how you're feeling—maybe they're words like *lost, confused, scared, small*—just silently acknowledge to yourself, *Yep, I'm feeling lost right now. I'm feeling scared. I don't know what to do.* Notice how it feels to lovingly acknowledge the part of you that wants to hide or freeze rather than to force it into action. Tell this part of you that you are here with it, that you are on the same side.

3. Use your breath to reassure this part of you that, indeed, this is not a time to take any action and that it is perfectly safe to rest in non-action. Give yourself permission to let it all go.

4. Remind yourself that you are deserving of your own time and attention and see how generously you can give both to yourself. Send love and soothing energy to yourself, as you would to a beloved child. Acknowledge the wisdom of taking this conscious time-out so as not to create even more unwanted momentum.

5. If possible, follow this process with a slow walk or a few minutes of journaling to help you sort through any insights or clarity that arose from within.

PROCESS 4: SOOTHING YOUR BODY'S FAWN RESPONSE—RELEASING PEOPLE-PLEASING

There are two keys to releasing the tendency toward fawning: The first is to call back from all other people the energy we have given to them in hopes that they will take care of us in return. The second is to remember that our happiness, well-being, and value are not dependent on any other human being, and it is our own responsibility to fill ourselves up from the inside out. The following process will guide you through these steps.

1. Begin by getting comfortable in a place where you're unlikely to be disturbed for the next few minutes. Then close your eyes and take a few long, slow, deep breaths.

2. Gently introduce the intention to become free from any survival tendency to fawn, to abandon your own needs and desires in order to please someone else. Call forth the intention to know and feel yourself as a powerful, independent being, free to express yourself completely, to take up as much space as you require, and to attract to yourself everything you desire, without explanation or apology.

3. With each inhalation, imagine calling your energy back from everyone and everything in the manifested world, past, present, or future. Visualize any part of your energy that is being used to fund someone else's vision or to uphold anyone else's well-being and see it now being returned to you. Remind yourself that each of us is a divine child of this universe, and each of us is connected to the powerful current of energy that sources all things. You are seeking only to strengthen your own relationship with Source and allow others to do likewise.

Appendix

4. As you feel your energy being returned to you, feel yourself standing within your own bubble of light that connects you directly to Source energy. You can picture this as your own circle of light that represents your inherent right to follow your heart, honor your desires, speak your mind, and create the life you desire.

5. Imagine this sphere of light getting brighter and brighter, dissolving any unhealthy entanglements or attachments between yourself and the people in your life. As these entanglements or cords of attachments burn away, feel the energy that was once flowing through them being returned to you. Allow any energy that belongs to others to gently and lovingly be returned to them as well.

6. If possible, I highly recommend doing something really nice for yourself—a slow walk, a hot bath, or spending some time outside in nature—as a way to integrate the energetic changes that have taken place.

Section 4: Energy Mastery Processes for Increasing Spiritual Flow

PROCESS 1: A TREATMENT FOR UNCONDITIONAL SELF-LOVE

Treatments have come to be a powerful practice that I share in my coaching sessions and workshops. Treatments are powerful prayers.

A spiritual treatment consists of five distinct statements or declarations:

1. *The Divine is* . . . The treatment begins with a general statement that acknowledges the presence of divine energy or a higher power, whether you refer to this power as God, Source, the Universe, or any other name. For example, *The Divine is abundant, powerful, and all-providing.*

2. *I am* . . . This statement brings your own self-identity into focus for the purpose of affirming who you are,

Appendix

what you believe, and what you now desire to manifest in your life. For example, *I am also abundant, powerful, and provided for.*

3. *I accept* or *I refuse* . . . In making this declaration, you are choosing either to accept or to reject certain thoughts, beliefs, or experiences. For example, *I refuse to focus on a lack of support, and I accept the support of the Divine.*

4. *I give thanks for* . . . With this statement, you are expressing your gratitude and appreciation for the many blessings and positive aspects of your life, and in so doing, you are further surrounding and magnetizing to yourself greater abundance and well-being. For example, *I give thanks for knowing I am supported. I am grateful for my life and for all the blessings in my life. I am grateful to be alive.*

5. *And so it is* . . . With this final declaration, you are sealing in the treatment, affirming that your desired outcome has already been fulfilled in the spiritual realm and is now in the process of manifesting in the material world.

With this understanding in mind, here is a spiritual treatment for unconditional self-love:

1. Affirm what you already know to be true about divine energy and the source of flow. For example, *The Divine is love, light, and life. The Divine is for me. The Divine is with me always.*

2. Declare what you are. For example, *I am one with this love, light, and life. I am supported. I am loved.*

Appendix

3. Make a choice, either to give up something that no longer serves you or to embody a vibration consistent with unconditional self-love. For example, *I accept that I am loved. I no longer accept the belief that I am not enough or that I am unlovable. I accept that I can create the life I want, as well as the forms I want to create. I now, in this moment, refuse to allow any self-hatred, self-criticism, self-judgment, or self-disapproval. I accept unconditional love and self-approval. I accept that compassion is a choice, as is judgment. I accept that I am perfect, whole, and complete as I am right now.*

4. Give thanks for whatever blessings or positive aspects you are most aware of in this moment. For example, *I give thanks for all the wonderful people, things, and opportunities in my life. I give thanks for the love that exists for me right now. I give thanks that unconditional love is here for me now. I give thanks knowing that I have the power to change anything in my life that doesn't feel good.*

5. Declare it complete. For example, *I declare unconditional love is my new agreement with myself. And so it is.*

PROCESS 2: BECOMING A CONDUIT FOR DIVINE ENERGY

Divine energy is the universal life force that exists everywhere and in everything, animating all of existence. Because we are all part of this energy stream, we do not have to work hard to connect with it. We only need to relax, allow, and let it flow to us and through us.

1. Begin by relaxing your body in preparation for this journey into becoming a conduit for divine energy.

2. Acknowledge the brilliance of your beautiful mind as you imagine divine light pouring down through the top of your head, filling up your mind and brain, and continuing through your spinal cord. Feel your entire central nervous system being called to relax and release anything unnecessary it may be holding on to.

3. Feel this pure, soothing, high-vibration light energy moving down though your nerves and limbic system and into your blood flow.

4. Taking another deep breath, allow yourself to feel the light moving into every cell. Imagine that each and every cell in your body is a tiny little cup, and they are being filled up with divine light.

5. Allow this energy to move into your heart center and feel your heart fill up with light.

6. Allow your awareness to rest now in the area around your heart. There is a lotus flower in the center of your heart, and it is blooming and opening. It is responding to the presence of this divine light as a flower responds to the sun.

7. Imagine your heart being filled with and overflowing with the light that is now flowing out and into every part of your body. Feel this beautiful energy moving down into the center of your emotional body, your lower belly. Allow your belly to fill with this light energy as you take a deep breath all the way down. Just as you filled up your heart center

Appendix

with light, imagine now that your emotional center is being filled up as well.

8. Now this light is fully surrounding your entire physical body and radiating out from you, expanding five feet in all directions.

9. Finally, as you recognize yourself as the conduit for this divine energy, allow yourself to flow and direct this energy out into every other aspect of your life . . . your relationships, your career, your finances, projects, travel plans, and so on. See each area being nourished and strengthened.

PROCESS 3: SETTING YOUR VIBRATIONAL TONE

Your personal vibration falls along a spectrum, just like the tones sounded by different keys on a piano, or the variations of the shades of light in a rainbow. Joy has a different tone than sadness; compassion has a different tone than anger. This process will support you in setting your vibrational tone intentionally.

1. Begin by reminding yourself that there is an unlimited amount of energy and light in this universe and that the same energy that created the sun and the stars is animating the atoms in your body. Everything is energy, and you are a part of it all.

Appendix

2. Allow yourself to visualize this universal energy and light as positive and unlimited and affirm that you can access as much of it as you allow yourself to. It is all for you.

3. Remember that you can choose your vibration the same way you choose a snack or a drink. So, imagine going up to this cosmic vending machine and declaring what you desire your "vibrational snack" to be. You have access to all the frequencies in the universe—you just need to point at the one you desire and pull the lever, so to speak. The full supply of that frequency is available to you now, as the vibration of your choosing. As you focus on it, it becomes reality.

4. Take a deep breath and ask yourself, *What vibration do I choose to reside within today?* Listen and feel for the answer. For example, *Today I choose the vibration of love. Today I choose freedom. Today I choose celebration.*

5. Allow all the energetic components of that vibration to flow from the universe to you, and feel it filling up your entire mind, your body, your emotions, and the energy field that surrounds you.

6. When you walk, feel as if you are walking within a vortex of this vibration.

7. When you speak, feel as though your thoughts and your words are being sourced by this vibration.

8. As you move through your day, reconnect as often as you like and fill yourself up anew with the vibration of your choosing.

PROCESS 4: A TOOL FOR EVERYDAY LIVING: STOP, OBSERVE, AND FLOW

In chapter 2, we explored how our instinctive, knee-jerk reaction when we perceive something is to form a conclusion about that situation, circumstance, or event as being either good or bad, wanted or unwanted. In other words, we make a personal judgment about what's happening, which then triggers a certain set of thoughts and emotions, which lead us to speak and behave in ways that are consistent with that mental and emotional state. This process works to our benefit when we're perceiving something that pleases us, but it works to our detriment when we're observing something that is other than the way we desire it to be.

For example, I observe that I don't have enough money in my bank account to pay my current bills. If I choose to interpret this as bad, my judgment will trigger a cascade of bad-feeling thoughts and emotions. I might feel angry, fearful, or anything between. I might blame some outside force, like my employer or the government, or I might turn the criticism upon myself. For example, *I'm so bad with money. What is wrong with me? Why can't I seem to make enough money to live the way I want to? I guess I'm not meant to be happy, rich, and successful after all.* My consciousness is now resonating with the lower-frequency vibrations such as fear, worry, resignation, and desperation, which then urge me to take actions that feel appropriate to that level of consciousness.

Appendix

This final process is designed to create space at each critical step of this progression so that you have a greater ability to choose in the direction of flow, especially with regards to the aspects of your life that you don't currently feel good about. When most of us were kids, we learned to stop, drop, and roll in case of fire. This process guides us—in the face of resistance—to stop, observe, and flow with compassion.

1. **Observe the facts of this situation.** Imagine that you are a lawyer whose job is to report only the facts, without any emotion, bias, or interpretation. What are the facts about what you are observing?

2. **Choose compassion rather than judgment.** Recognize that if you make the choice to judge what you're observing, it will sound something like *This is bad*, or *I am screwed*, and will lead only to greater resistance and pain if you don't flow. So, make the choice to give yourself compassion. Close your eyes, take some deep breaths, and send compassion to yourself for being in this unwanted situation. Feel yourself filling up with soothing, healing light.

3. **Visualize your preferred reality.** Ask yourself, *If I had a magic wand, how would I like this contrasting situation to be?* For example, *I desire all my bills to be paid, on time, with money left over.* Activate your mental body by visualizing yourself in this different or better experience.

4. **Connect to the essence of what you desire.** Ask yourself, *Why would I want this new situation? How would I feel if this were already my reality?* For example, I *want to feel good, abundant, at peace, in flow!* Activate your emotional body by

feeling the essence of your desire as if it were a reality now.

5. **Allow yourself to feel the flow** of this new, desired vibration filling every aspect of your consciousness: your mind, emotions, physical body, and energetic body. Allow this vibration to grow and expand until it radiates from and around you like an aura, filling your entire energy body, five feet above, below, around, and within.

6. **You are now back in the flow.** Rinse and repeat as often as needed. Observe the ups and downs of your life without judgment. Simply allow your desired energy to flow without your mind making any situation wrong or bad.

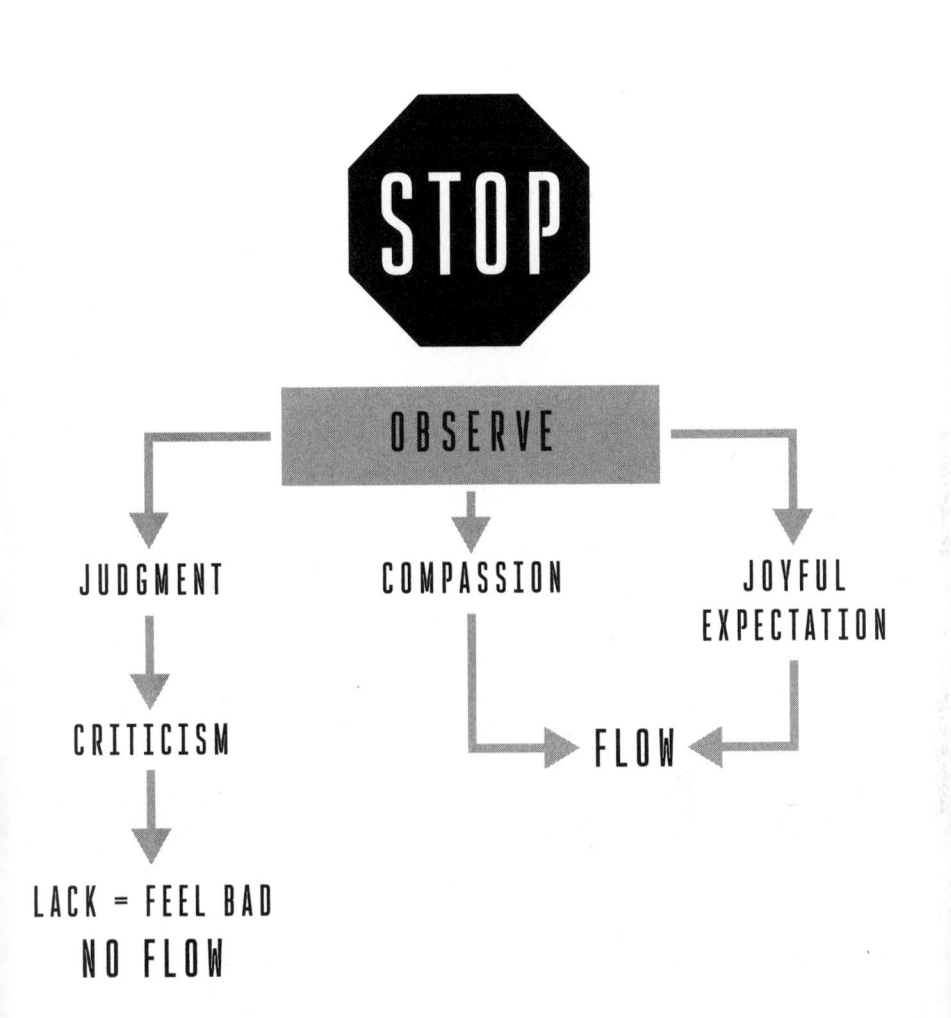

Appendix

STOP

OBSERVE

- JUDGMENT → CRITICISM → LACK = FEEL BAD / NO FLOW
- COMPASSION → FLOW
- JOYFUL EXPECTATION → FLOW

RESOURCES

The insights and tools shared throughout this book have shown you many ways to return to a state of flow rather than allowing your survival instincts to take over in moments of tension or emotional distress. If you desire additional support in shifting reactive patterns within yourself that are negatively affecting your relationships, finances, creativity, or physical health, the first resource I would guide you toward is The Quantum Council of Light. The Council has the advantage of knowing what you are asking for at the level of intention, what energetic blocks currently exist between you and your desires, and which universal laws can best guide you along the path of least resistance toward greater flow and freedom in each important aspect of your life. The Council offers group and individual sessions, both live/in-person and virtual. To schedule your Freedom and Flow Session or to discover upcoming programs and workshops, please visit christywhitman.com.

I also want to acknowledge that individuals who have experienced significant trauma may benefit from specialized support that is outside the scope of what the Council provides and what I have presented in this book. In these cases, seeking professional help can be a crucial and extremely beneficial step toward healing, inner peace, and energy mastery. The following resources are provided as a starting point for dealing with complex trauma. Please note that this list is not exhaustive, and it's essential to consult with your mental health professional to develop a personalized treatment plan.

DOMESTIC VIOLENCE / SEXUAL ASSAULT

- National Domestic Violence Hotline: 800-799-SAFE (800-799-7233) thehotline.org/help
  Supports anyone experiencing domestic violence or questioning unhealthy aspects of their relationship.

- National Sexual Assault Hotline 800-656-HOPE (800-656-4673) rainn.org
  A free, confidential 24/7 phone service and chat line offering support to survivors and their loved ones.

NATURAL DISASTERS AND OTHER TRAUMAS

- Disaster Distress Helpline: (800-985-5990) samhsa.gov/find-help/disaster-distress-helpline
  Counselors are available 24/7 to offer support to those who need crisis counseling after experiencing a traumatic event or disaster.

- VictimConnect: 855-4-VICTIM (855-484-2846) victimconnect.org
  Offers confidential support and referrals for crime victims.

Resources

- National Human Trafficking Hotline: (888-373-7888) humantraffickinghotline.org
  Provides resources, referrals, and other support for victims of human trafficking.

- National Suicide Prevention Lifeline: Call or Text 988 suicidepreventionlifeline.org
  Offers free and confidential support for people in distress and prevention and crisis resources for loved ones.

VETERANS AND PTSD

- U.S. Department of Veterans Affairs: 800-MyVA411 (800-698-2411) va.gov/health-care/health-needs-conditions/mental-health/ptsd
  Provides support, education, and practical help for those who have survived war, disasters, or mass violence.

CHILDREN AND PARENTS

- ChildHelp 800-4-A-CHILD (800-422-4453) childhelp.org
  Provides support, education and counseling to child abuse victims, parents, and concerned individuals.

- National Parent Helpline: 855-4-A-PARENT (855-427-2736) parentsanonymous.org/helplines/
  Provides emotional support and resources to parents and caregivers.

Resources

LGBTQIA+

- Trevor Lifeline: 866-488-7386
  thetrevorproject.org
  Provides support for LGBTQIA+ youth who are in crisis, feeling suicidal, or in need of a safe and judgment-free place to talk.

SELECTED BIBLIOGRAPHY

The Cleveland Clinic. "Limbic System" https://my.clevelandclinic.org/health/body/limbic-system.

Daum, Kevin. "These 37 Quotes by Mahatma Gandhi Will Help You Find Inner Peace in Turbulent Times." Inc.com. October 2, 2019. https://www.inc.com/kevin-daum/these-37-quotes-by-mahatma-gandhi-will-help-you-find-inner-peace-in-turbulent-times.html.

Frankl, Viktor E. *Man's Search for Meaning.* Simon & Schuster, 1959.

Hebb, Donald Olding. *The Organization of Behavior: A Neuropsychological Theory.* Psychology Press, 2012.

Selected Bibliography

Hicks, Esther and Jerry Hicks. *Ask and It Is Given: Learning to Manifest Your Desires*. Hay House, 2004.

Jung, Carl Gustav. *Christ: A Symbol of the Self*. Princeton University Press, 1958.

Jung, Carl Gustav. *Memories, Dreams, Reflections*. Vintage Books, 1989.

Karpman, Stephen. "Fairy Tales and Script Drama Analysis," *The Transactional Analysis Bulletin* 7, no. 26 (1968): 39–43, https://calisphere.org/item/52ceb48d-c76a-4df3-934d-88d7096f3b29.

Karpman, Stephen. *A Game Free Life: Living Beyond the Ego*. Hay House, 2014.

Maitreya, Ananda. *The Dhammapada*. Parallax Press, 2001.

Schucman, Helen. *A Course in Miracles*. Foundation for Inner Peace, 1976.

Scovel Shinn, Florence. *Your Word Is Your Wand*. Hay House, 2006. Originally published in 1928.

Shapiro, Francine. *Getting Past Your Past*. TarcherPerigee, 2018.

Walker, Pete. *Complex PTSD: From Surviving to Thriving*. Routledge, 2013.

Walling, Peter T. "An Update on Dimensions of Consciousness," *Baylor University Medical Center Proceedings* 33, no. 1: 126–30. https://doi.org/10.1080/08998280.2019.1656009.

Winfrey, Oprah and Bruce Perry. *What Happened to You?* Flatiron Books, 2021.

ACKNOWLEDGMENTS

I acknowledge all my amazing clients who are part of the Energy Vortex Community at christywhitman.com whom I get to connect with and support each day. I applaud your courage, willingness, and dedication to your own path of light and flow. You are my heroes, and your transformation is my greatest gift. Thank you.

I acknowledge my father, Frank, who passed in 2024. Thank you for showing me what contrast and resistance to life looks like. You are and will forever be my greatest teacher. I would not have learned flow if it wasn't for you and Mom.

To my editor, Danielle Dorman, the team at Beyond Words Publishing, and my own entire team, who help me do what I do each and every day. It takes an incredible support system to be able to serve in the way that I do. I appreciate each one of you.

To my husband . . . my greatest gift, who is there for me even when I am not in flow. And to Alex and Max, who keep me humble, grounded, and always laughing. I appreciate and love each one of you deeply. THANK YOU. :)

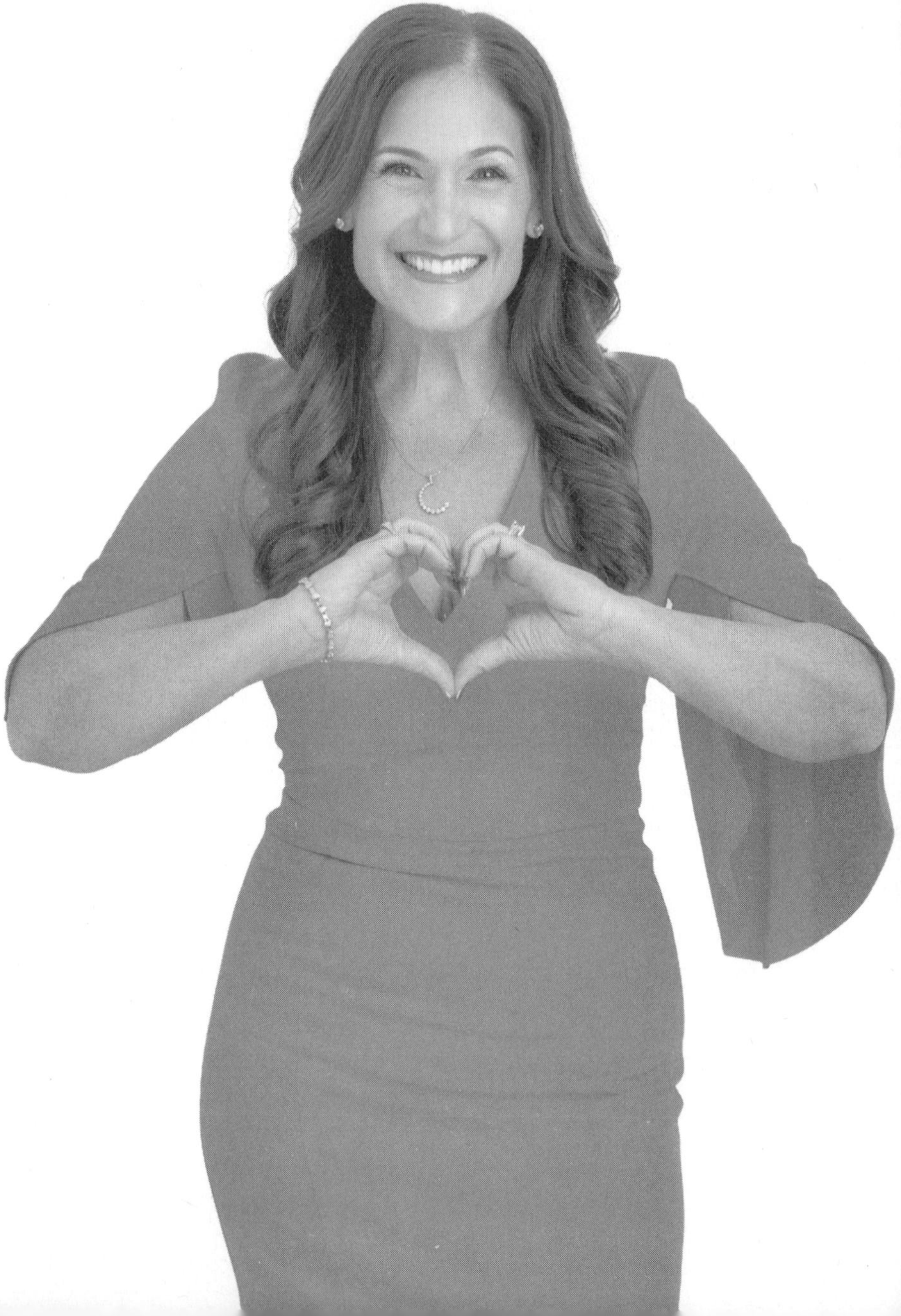

ABOUT THE AUTHOR

Christy Whitman is a transformational leader, celebrity coach, Law of Attraction expert, and the author of the international bestsellers *The Desire Factor* and *Quantum Success* and the *New York Times* bestselling books *The Art of Having It All* and *Taming Your Alpha Bitch.*

Christy has appeared on numerous media outlets, including *The Today Show, The Morning Show,* TedX, and the Hallmark Channel. She and her work have been featured in various publications, including Goalcast, *People, Seventeen, Woman's Day, Hollywood Life,* and *Teen Vogue,* to name a few.

Christy is the CEO and founder of the Quantum Success Coaching Academy, an online Law of Attraction coaching certification program. She has helped certify over three thousand life coaches and has helped countless others unlock their power to manifest. Christy is also the channel for a group of ascended masters who call themselves The Quantum Council of Light, or the Council.